Algebra

Test your knowledge

15 minutes

1
a) Solve the equations giving your answer to two decimal places where appropriate:

  i) $x^2 - 6x + 8 = 0$ ii) $2x^2 - x = 1$ iii) $x^2 - x - 1 = 0$.

b) Factorise:

  i) $x^2 - 5x - 24$ ii) $2x^2 + 11x + 12$ iii) $4x^2 + 39x - 10$.

2 Solve:

  a) $(x - 7)(2x + 3) = (1 - 4x)(x + 9)$.   b) $\dfrac{1}{x} + \dfrac{2}{x-1} = \dfrac{5}{2}$.   c) $\dfrac{x+2}{3x-4} = \dfrac{x}{2x-3}$.

3
a) Without a calculator, find the following, expressing your answers as fractions:

  i) 4^{-2} ii) $1000^{1/3}$ iii) $9^{-3/2}$.

b) Solve the following equations:

  i) $2^{3x+2} = 256$ ii) $\frac{1}{9} = 3^{x-3}$.

c) Simplify the following: $\dfrac{\sqrt{(8a^3)}(\sqrt{b})^4}{(4ab)^{1.5}}$.

4
a) Solve the following inequalities:

  i) $3x + 6 \leqslant 21$ ii) $4 - 6x \leqslant 1$ iii) $2x + 6 > 3x + 2$.

b) Write down the integer values for which the following inequalities are satisfied:

  i) $-5 < 3x - 2 \leqslant 10$ ii) $x + 4 \leqslant 3 - 4x$ and $x > -5$.

Answers

b) i) 0, 1, 2, 3, 4 ii) −4, −3, −2, −1
c) $b^{0.5} 2^{-1.5}$ 4 a) i) $x \geqslant 5$ ii) $x \geqslant \frac{1}{2}$ iii) $x > 4$
3 a) i) $\frac{1}{16}$ ii) 10 iii) $\frac{1}{27}$ b) i) $x = 2$ ii) $x = 1$
b) $x = 2$; c) $x = \frac{5}{3}$; $x = 2$; x = 3$
(iii) $(4x - 1)(x + 10)$ 2 a) $x = 1$; $x = -5$
$x = -0.62$ b) i) $(x - 8)(x + 3)$ ii) $(2x + 3)(x + 4)$
1.62; iii) $x = 1$; $x = -\frac{1}{2}$ ii) $x = 4$ iii) $x = 2$; $x = 1.62$;

If you got them all right, skip to page 10

1

Algebra

Improve your knowledge

40 minutes

1 A **quadratic equation** is an equation with x^2 in it somewhere – like $x^2 + 3x - 4 = 0$. You need to be able to factorise and solve these equations.

There are many different methods for factorising, but we will be using a 'cheat' method that always works. It involves using the **quadratic equation formula** (on your formula sheet) which you have to be able to use anyway:

$$x = \frac{-b \pm \sqrt{(b^2 - 4ac)}}{2a}$$

where the 'general' quadratic equation is $ax^2 + bx + c = 0$.

You must have 0 on one side!

Let's see how to use this to solve equations first.

Example 1

Solve $2x^2 + 6 = 7x$.

Step 1 Make sure equation has 0 on one side, and the other side has the x^2 term, then the x term, then the number.

Need to bring the $7x$ over:
$2x^2 + 6 - 7x = 0$

Re-arrange:
$2x^2 - 7x + 6 = 0$

Be careful with minus signs!

Step 2 Write down what a, b and c are equal to.

$a = 2$, $b = -7$, $c = 6$

Step 3 Write down the formula, putting in your values of a, b and c. Remember '4ac' means '4 × a × c'.

$$x = \frac{--7 \pm \sqrt{[(-7)^2 - 4 \times 2 \times 6]}}{2 \times 2}$$

Remember – if you square a minus number, you get a plus.

Don't try to simplify **yet!**

Step 4 Work out the bracket inside the square root.

$$x = \frac{--7 \pm \sqrt{[49 - 48]}}{2 \times 2}$$

so $x = \dfrac{--7 \pm \sqrt{1}}{2 \times 2}$

Step 5 Work out the square root and do other easy simplifications.

$$x = \frac{7 \pm 1}{4}$$

since $--7 = +7$, and $\sqrt{1} = 1$

Step 6 Separate the $\pm$ into + or −.

$$x = \frac{7+1}{4} \text{ or } x = \frac{7-1}{4}.$$

so $x = 2$ or $1\frac{1}{2}$

Now we need to know how to use the formula to help us to factorise equations, i.e. put them into brackets.

Example 2 Factorise $2x^2 - 7x + 6$

Step 1 Solve the equation using the formula, getting your answers as fractions, not decimals.

We did this one earlier, and got $x = 2$ and $x = 1\frac{1}{2}$

Step 2 Write down:
$(x - 1^{st}$ root$)(x - 2^{nd}$ root$)$.

$(x - 2)(x - 1\frac{1}{2})$

Step 3 If a bracket has got a fraction in it, multiply the whole bracket by the bottom of the fraction.

$(x - 1\frac{1}{2})$ has a fraction in it. The bottom of the fraction is 2, so multiply by 2:
$2(x - 1\frac{1}{2}) = 2x - 3$

Step 4 Write down your new brackets. If you've got time, multiply out to check it's right.

$(x - 2)(2x - 3)$

$2x^2 - 3x - 4x + 6 \equiv 2x^2 - 7x + 6 \checkmark$

Example 3 Factorise $3x^2 + 5x - 2$.

Solution Although this has not got an $=$ sign, we can still treat it the same way:

$$a = 3; b = 5; c = -2 \implies x = \frac{-5 \pm \sqrt{[(5)^2 - 4 \times 3 \times -2]}}{2 \times 3} = \frac{-5 \pm \sqrt{[25--24]}}{2 \times 3}$$

$$= \frac{-5 \pm \sqrt{[49]}}{2 \times 3} = \frac{-5 \pm 7}{6}$$

So $x = \frac{-5+7}{6}$ or $x = \frac{-5-7}{6}$ so $x = \frac{2}{6} = \frac{1}{3}$ or $x = -2$

So our brackets are: $(x - \frac{1}{3})(x - -2) \Rightarrow (x - \frac{1}{3})(x + 2)$

Multiplying $(x - \frac{1}{3})$ by 3, we get $3x - 1$, so our brackets are: $(3x - 1)(x + 2)$

Multiplying out to check: $(3x - 1)(x + 2) \equiv 3x^2 + 6x - x - 2 \equiv 3x^2 + 5x - 2\checkmark$

2 There are quite a lot of harder-looking equations that simplify down to quadratics. The key idea is to get all the terms on one side.

Example 4 Solve the equation $(2x - 3)(x - 3) = (3x - 1)(6 - x)$.

Solution We know this will eventually turn into a quadratic because if we multiplied out the brackets we'd get x^2s. Since we want to get it all on one side, we need to multiply out each side:

$$(2x - 3)(x - 3) \equiv 2x^2 - 6x - 3x + 9 \equiv 2x^2 - 9x + 9$$

$$(3x - 1)(6 - x) \equiv 18x - 3x^2 - 6 + x \equiv 19x - 3x^2 - 6$$

So $2x^2 - 9x + 9 = 19x - 3x^2 - 6$

Now we have to get them all on one side:

$2x^2 - 9x + 9 - 19x + 3x^2 + 6 = 0$ Simplifying: $5x^2 - 28x + 15 = 0$

Now we can solve it!

$$x = \frac{- -28 \pm \sqrt{[(-28)^2 - 4 \times 5 \times 15]}}{2 \times 5} = \frac{- -28 \pm \sqrt{[784 - 300]}}{2 \times 5}$$

$$= \frac{28 \pm 22}{10} = \frac{50}{10} \text{ or } \frac{6}{10} = 5 \text{ or } \frac{3}{5}.$$

Algebraic Fractions

You may get equations containing fractions with letters in them – like:

$$\frac{2}{x} - \frac{4x}{2x + 1} = 3.$$

Just like normal fractions, the first thing you do is put them over a common denominator! After that, you cross-multiply. You should end up with a quadratic.

Example 5 Solve

$$\frac{2}{x} - \frac{4x}{2x + 1} = 3.$$

Solution

We need to put $\dfrac{2}{x}$ and $\dfrac{4x}{2x+1}$

> Careful with multiplying out – make sure you use brackets.

over a common denominator. To find it, we just multiply together the bottoms of the fractions – so common denominator is $x \times (2x+1) = 2x^2 + x$.

Now multiply the top of each fraction by the bottom of the other one, and put them over the common denominator:

So $\dfrac{2}{x} - \dfrac{4x}{2x+1} = \dfrac{2(2x+1) - 4x(x)}{2x^2+x}$

Now multiply out the top and simplify:

$$\frac{2}{x} - \frac{4x}{2x+1} = \frac{2(2x+1) - 4x(x)}{2x^2+x} = \frac{4x+2-4x^2}{2x^2+x}$$

Now go back to the original equation:

$$\frac{2}{x} - \frac{4x}{2x+1} = 3 \implies \frac{4x+2-4x^2}{2x^2+x} = 3$$

Now cross-multiply:

$$\frac{4x+2-4x^2}{2x^2+x} = 3 \implies 4x+2-4x^2 = 3 \times (2x^2+x)$$

Simplify and take all over to one side:

$$4x+3-4x^2 = 6x^2+3x \implies 0 = 6x^2+3x-4x-3+4x^2 \implies 10x^2-x-3 = 0$$

Now solve as normal:

$$a = 10;\, b = -1;\, c = -3 \implies x = \frac{--1 \pm \sqrt{[(-1)^2 - 4 \times 10 \times -3]}}{2 \times 10}$$

$$\implies x = \frac{1 \pm 11}{20} \implies x = \frac{12}{20} \text{ or } -\frac{10}{20} \quad \text{So } x = \frac{3}{5} \text{ or } -\frac{1}{2}.$$

3 From Intermediate maths, you should already know things like $y^3 = y \times y \times y$; $2^5 = 2 \times 2 \times 2 \times 2 \times 2$.

For Higher maths, you also have to deal with **negative** and **fraction powers**. You should learn:

Work out 2^5 on your calculator by doing $2y^x5$.

Anything to the power 0 is 1.

Anything to the power 1 is the number itself: $5^1 = 5$.

A **negative** power means 'one over': $x^{-3} = \dfrac{1}{x^3}$.

A **fraction** power means roots: $x^{1/2} = \sqrt{x}$; $x^{1/3} = \sqrt[3]{x}$; $x^{3/2} = \sqrt{x^3}$ or $(\sqrt{x})^3$.

Questions may ask you to use these facts to work out powers of numbers without a calculator – in other words, showing all your working (although you can still use your calculator to check).

Example 6 Without a calculator, find the following:

      a) $4^{3/2}$

      b) $100^{-3/2}$.

Solution

a) $4^{3/2} = \sqrt{(4^3)} = \sqrt{(4 \times 4 \times 4)} = \sqrt{64} = 8$.

b) Negative powers tells us 'one over':

$$100^{-3/2} = \frac{1}{100^{3/2}} = \frac{1}{\sqrt{100^3}} = \frac{1}{\sqrt{1,000,000}} = \frac{1}{1000}.$$

You also need to know the laws of powers, which are:

$y^m \times y^n = y^{m+n}$ i.e. 'If you're multiplying, add the powers'

$y^m \div y^n = y^{m-n}$ i.e. 'If you're dividing, subtract the powers'

$(y^m)^n = y^{mn}$ i.e. 'If you've got a power of a power, multiply'

You must be **very** careful using these laws.

- You can't use them to deal with something like $2^4 \times 5^3$, because you **must** have the same base for each power.

- You can expand brackets like $(2x)^3 = 2^3 \times x^3 = 8x^3$, or $\sqrt{\dfrac{3}{x}} = \dfrac{\sqrt{3}}{\sqrt{x}}$.

- You can't easily expand brackets with + or − in them, i.e. you can't do anything to simplify $\sqrt{(x + y)}$ or $(2x - 1)^{-2}$.

Questions may ask you to use your knowledge of powers to solve equations, or to simplify something.

If you're solving equations, you need to get both sides as powers of a simple number (like 2, 3, 5 ...), then use the laws of powers. If stuck, use trial and error!

Example 7   Solve the equation: $2^{x+1} = \frac{1}{8}$

Solution

a) We need to get both sides as powers of the same number. 2 is the obvious one, since one side is already a power of 2, and we know $8 = 2 \times 2 \times 2 = 2^3$. So we must convert $\frac{1}{8}$ to a power of 2. Since $8 = 2^3$,

$$\frac{1}{8} = \frac{1}{2^3} = 2^{-3}$$

('one over' means powers are negative)

So $2^{x+1} = \frac{1}{8} \Longrightarrow 2^{x+1} = 2^{-3}$

If these are equal, we must have $x + 1 = -3$ so $x = -4$.

If you're simplifying powers, try the following strategies:

- Don't try to do everything at once – work out one bit at a time.
- Convert $\sqrt{}$ symbols to the appropriate powers first.
- Then open out brackets: $(2x)^4 = 2^4 x^4$ and $(x^{-3})^2 = x^{-3 \times 2} = x^{-6}$.
- Collect terms – all numbers together, all powers of the same letter together – by using laws of powers.
- If it's a fraction, work on the numerator and denominator separately at first, then combine them, remembering you're dividing, so subtract powers.
- Check your calculations involving numbers on the calculator.

Example 8   Simplify the following: $\dfrac{(3a)^{-1}(2b^2)^{3/2}}{\sqrt{2}ab}$.

Solution

Convert √ to a power:

$$\frac{(3a)^{-1}(2b^2)^{3/2}}{\sqrt{2}ab} = \frac{(3a)^{-1}(2b^2)^{3/2}}{2^{1/2}ab}$$

Open out brackets:

$$(3a)^{-1} = 3^{-1}a^{-1} \qquad (2b^2)^{3/2} = 2^{3/2}(b^2)^{3/2} = 2^{3/2}b^{2(3/2)} = 2^{3/2}b^3$$

So we have

$$\frac{(3a)^{-1}(2b^2)^{3/2}}{2^{1/2}ab} = \frac{3^{-1}a^{-1}2^{3/2}b^3}{2^{1/2}ab}$$

Combine numerator and denominator.

Look at each type of term individually:

$$a^{-1}/a = a^{-1}/a^1 = a^{-1-1} = a^{-2} \qquad b^3/b = b^3/b^1 = b^{3-1} = b^2$$

$2^{3/2}/2^{1/2} = 2^{3/2-1/2} = 2^1 = 2$.
There is no 3 in the denominator, so we just have $3^{-1} = \frac{1}{3}$.

So altogether we have

$$3^{-1}a^{-2}b^2 2 = \frac{2b^2}{3a^2}.$$

> NEGATIVE powers means they go on the bottom.

Inequalities

Inequalities are things with $<$, $\leqslant$, $>$, $\geqslant$ in them instead of an $=$ sign. The 'open end' points towards the larger number – so $3 > 2$ is read '3 is greater than 2' and $x \leqslant 4$ is read 'x is less than or equal to 4'.

You deal with inequalities rather like you deal with equations, but you must remember:

- You can **add** or **subtract** anything to or from either side.
- You can **multiply** or **divide** by **positive** numbers.
- You can **multiply** or **divide** by **negative** numbers, provided you **change the direction of the sign**.
- You cannot do anything else!

> You may find it easier if you AVOID multiplying or dividing by negative numbers

You can be asked to solve an inequality, which will leave you with an answer like (say) $x \leqslant 2$, or you can be asked to list whole-number values it is true for.

Example 9

    a)   Solve the inequalities:

        i) $4 + 2x \leqslant 10$

        ii) $6x - 2 < 18 - 4x.$

    b)   List the integer values of x for which the following hold:

        i) $2 \leqslant 2x - 6 < 10$

        ii) $1 - x < x + 5$ and $x < 3.$

Solution

a)   i) $4 + 2x \leqslant 10$

          Take the 4 over: $2x \leqslant 10 - 4 \Rightarrow 2x \leqslant 6$

          Divide by 2: $x \leqslant 3.$

     ii) $6x - 2 < 18 - 4x$

          Bring the $4x$ over: $6x + 4x - 2 < 18 \Rightarrow 10x - 2 < 18$

          Take the 2 over: $10x < 18 + 2 \Rightarrow 10x < 20$

          Divide by 10: $x < 2.$

b)   i)   Get x on its own first: $2 \leqslant 2x - 6 < 10$

          Add 6 to everything: $2 + 6 \leqslant 2x - 6 + 6 < 10 + 6 \Rightarrow 8 \leqslant 2x < 16$

          Divide by 2: $4 \leqslant x < 8$

So we want values greater than or equal to 4, but less than 8: these are 4, 5, 6, 7.

     ii) $1 - x < x + 5 \Rightarrow 1 < 2x + 5 \Rightarrow -4 < 2x \Rightarrow -2 < x$

So we have $-2 < x$ and $x < 3$ so $x = -1, 0, 1, 2.$

Now learn how to use your knowledge

Algebra

Use your knowledge

30 minutes

1 a) Factorise $6x^2 + x - 1$.   *Hint 1*

    b) Hence solve $6x^3 + x^2 - x = 0$.   *Hint 2*

2 a) Show that

$$\frac{1}{2(x-1)} - \frac{1}{2(x+1)} = \frac{1}{x^2 - 1}.$$ *Hint 3*

    b) Hence solve the equation

$$\frac{1}{2(x-1)} - \frac{1}{2(x+1)} = \frac{1}{8}.$$ *Hint 4*

3 Shakeel's rectangular lawn is 144 square feet in area. Its perimeter is 52 feet. Let L be the length of Shakeel's lawn, and W be its width.

    a) Use what you know about the lawn's perimeter to show $W = 26 - L$.   *Hint 5*

    b) Use the lawn's area to obtain another equation connecting L and W.   *Hint 6*

    c) Hence show that $L^2 - 26L + 144 = 0$.   *Hint 7*

    d) Solve this equation to find the length of the lawn.   *Hint 8*

4 Use the formula $s = ut + \frac{1}{2}at^2$ to find the possible values of t when $s = 5$, $u = 20$ and $a = -9.8$, giving your answer correct to two decimal places.   *Hint 9*

5 Show that:

i) $\frac{1}{81} = 3^{-4}$

Hint 10

ii) $3 \times 9^y = 3^{2y+1}$

Hint 11

iii) $27 \times 27^y = 3^{3y+3}$.

Hint 12

6 Solve the equations:

Hint 13

a) $x^{2/3} = 9$.

Hint 14

b) $x^{-3} = 64$.

7 I am thinking of a number. If you treble it and add 5, the result is less than 50.

If you double it and subtract the answer from 60, the result is less than 36.

a) Write down a pair of inequalities satisfied by my number.

Hint 15

b) Solve these inequalities.

c) Given that I am thinking of an integer, list the possible values my number can have.

Hint 16

Hints follow

Algebra

1 Get the solution as fractions and multiply each bracket by the denominator!

2 Take out a factor of x.

3 Common denominator, then look to try to cancel numbers.

4 Use what you've just done and cross multiply.

5 Find the perimeter in terms of W and L, put it equal to 52.

6 How do you work out the area of a rectangle?

7 Substitute the equation from a) into the equation from b) and simplify.

8 Find the roots and check what each gives for the width.

9 Substitute the numbers in, then re-arrange and use the formula.

10 Remember 'one over' means 'negative power'.

11 Use $9 = 3^2$ to work out 9^y in terms of 3.

12 Use $27 = 3^3$.

13 $x^{2/3} = \sqrt[3]{x^2}$.

14 Use $x^{-3} = \dfrac{1}{x^3}$, then re-arrange to find x.

15 Let the number be x. Work out what you get in each case in terms of x.

16 Which whole numbers are they both true for?

Answers on page 88

Rational and irrational numbers

10 minutes

Test your knowledge

1 Identify which of the following numbers are irrational:

   a) $\sqrt{5}$ b) $\sqrt{49}$ c) 2π d) $8 - \sqrt{2}$ e) $0.4\dot{5}$ f) $\frac{7}{8}$.

2 Change the following decimals to vulgar fractions:

   a) 0.0236 b) $0.\dot{4}$ c) $0.\dot{2}\dot{1}$.

3 Find a rational and an irrational number in between 0.5 and 0.6.

4 a) For each of the irrational numbers in this question, find an irrational number that when added to it produces a rational number:

   i) $2\sqrt{17}$ ii) $3 - 2\sqrt{5}$.

   b) For each of the irrational numbers in this question, find an irrational number that when multiplied by it produces a rational number:

   i) $2\sqrt{6}$ ii) $8 - \sqrt{7}$.

Answers

1 a), c), d) are irrational
2 a) $0.0236 = \frac{0236}{10000} = \frac{236}{10000} = \frac{59}{2500}$
   b) $x = \frac{4}{9}$ c) $x = \frac{7}{33}$
3 Rational: 0.55 irrational: $\sqrt{0.30}$ ($= 0.54772....$)
   but you may have different answers!
4 a) i) $2\sqrt{17} + (5 - 2\sqrt{17}) = 5$
   ii) $(3 - 2\sqrt{5}) + (3 + 2\sqrt{5}) = 6$
   b) i) $2\sqrt{6} \times (7\sqrt{6}) = 14$
   ii) $(8 - \sqrt{7}) \times (8 + \sqrt{7}) = 57$

If you got them all right, skip to page 17

13

Rational and irrational numbers

15 minutes

Improve your knowledge

1 A rational number is one that can be written as a fraction which cannot be cancelled any further. They include: any whole number (including zero and negatives), any decimal that does not go on for ever (i.e. terminates), and any recurring decimal.

An irrational number goes on for ever as a decimal without repeating itself exactly. They include numbers like $\pi = 3.1415926...$ and $\sqrt{2} = 1.41421356...$

[The **square root** of any number that **isn't** an **exact square** is **irrational**.]

> **Be careful!** Not all numbers written with square roots have to be irrational, e.g. $\sqrt{4} = 2$, which is not irrational.

Numbers like $3 \times \sqrt{5}$ and $2 + \pi$ are also irrational, because they have an 'irrational bit'.

2 You can **convert** any **normal** decimal (i.e. one that does not go on for ever) such as 0.00624 into a **fraction** by the following procedure:

- Count how many decimal places there are.

  For 0.00624 there are 5 decimal places.

- Put whatever's after the decimal point on top of 1 followed by that many zeros.

  $\frac{00624}{100000} = \frac{624}{100000}$ (5 zeros as 5 decimal places).

- Cancel if necessary.

  Divide top and bottom by 16: $\frac{39}{6250}$.

Example 1 shows how to convert recurring decimals to fractions:

Example 1 Express as fractions: a) $0.\dot{2}$ b) $0.\dot{6}\dot{7}$.

Solution

a) Let $x = 0.\dot{2} = 0.22222222...$ then $10x = 2.22222222....$

Now we subtract:
$10x - x = 2.22222222... - 0.22222222...$

But all the 2s after the decimal point
cancel so $9x = 2$ so $x = \frac{2}{9}$.

Multiply by 10 because one recurring figure.

b) Let $x = 0.\dot{6}\dot{7} = 0.676767....$
then $100\ x = 67.676767....$

Subtract:
$100x - x = 67.676767...-0.676767...$ so
$99x = 67$ so $x = \frac{67}{99}$.

Multiply by 100 because two recurring figures.

3 Questions sometimes ask you to **find** a **rational** and an **irrational** number **between** two other **numbers**. Example 2 shows you how to do this:

Example 2 Find a rational number and an irrational number between 4 and 4.1.

Solution For the rational number, we just choose a normal decimal: 4.05 will do. For the irrational:

Step 1 Square both numbers. $4^2 = 16$ $4.1^2 = 16.81$

Step 2 Choose any number between   Try 16.5: $\sqrt{16.5} = 4.062019...$ so
the two squares that you   16.5 is not a perfect square.
don't think is a perfect
square (take the square root
on your calculator to check).

Step 3 Write down $\sqrt{}$(this number)   So $\sqrt{16.5}$ is an irrational number
(don't work it out).   in between 4 and 4.1.

4 You may be asked to **find** an **irrational number** which, when **added/multiplied** by the **irrational number** given in the question, makes a **rational number**. Adding is shown in Example 3, while multiplying is shown in Example 4.

Example 3

a) Write down an irrational number which when added to $1 - \sqrt{27}$ produces a rational number.

b) Write down an irrational number which when added to $2\sqrt{3}$ produces a rational number.

Solution

a) We need something that will cancel out the $-\sqrt{27}$ so we use (any whole number) $+ \sqrt{27}$, e.g. $5 + \sqrt{27}$: $(1 - \sqrt{27}) + (5 + \sqrt{27}) = 6$.

b) We need to cancel out the $2\sqrt{3}$, so use (whole number) $-2\sqrt{3}$, e.g. $8 - 2\sqrt{3}$: $(2\sqrt{3}) + (8 - 2\sqrt{3}) = 8$.

Example 4

a) Which **different** irrational number when multiplied by $\sqrt{2}$ produces a rational number?

b) Which irrational number when multiplied by $5 + \sqrt{3}$, produces a rational number?

Solution

a) To cancel out the $\sqrt{2}$, we need to multiply by $\dfrac{\text{something}}{\sqrt{2}}$,

where 'something' is a whole number – say 3. So

$$\sqrt{2} \times \frac{3}{\sqrt{2}} = \frac{\sqrt{2}}{1} \times \frac{3}{\sqrt{2}} = \frac{3}{1} = 3.$$

b) This has to be treated differently; we use the result $(x - y)(x + y) = x^2 - y^2$. As we have $5 + \sqrt{3}$, we have to multiply by $5 - \sqrt{3}$ (i.e. we change the sign): $(5 + \sqrt{3})(5 - \sqrt{3}) = 5^2 - (\sqrt{3})^2 = 25 - 3 = 22$.

If we'd started with $5 - \sqrt{3}$, we'd be multiplying by $5 + \sqrt{3}$.

Now learn how to use your knowledge

Rational and irrational numbers

15 minutes

Use your knowledge

1 Express 0.2̇13̇ as a vulgar fraction.

Hints 1–2

2 For each of the irrational numbers in this question, find an irrational number that when multiplied by it, produces a rational number:

Hint 3

a) $6 - 2\sqrt{3}$ b) $\sqrt{7} + \sqrt{5}$ c) $\dfrac{1}{2 + \sqrt{6}}$.

3 Find a rational and an irrational number in between $\sqrt{2}$ and $\sqrt{3}$. *Hint 4*

4 State whether the following statements are always true(T), always false(F) or sometimes true and sometimes false(S). For any true statement, give an explanation. For any statement you think is false, give an example that shows why it is false. For any statement that is sometimes true and sometimes false, give an example of each.

a) Rational number + rational number = rational number.   *Hint 5*

b) Rational number × irrational number = rational number.   *Hint 6*

c) Irrational number × irrational number = irrational number.   *Hints 7–8*

d) Irrational number – irrational number = irrational number.   *Hint 9*

e) Irrational number² = rational number.   *Hint 10*

f) Rational number – rational number = rational number.   *Hint 11*

✓ *Hints follow*

Rational and irrational numbers

1   As there are three repeating digits, what do you think you should multiply by?

2   Multiply by 1000.

3   Just change the sign!

4   Find √2 and √3 on your calculator, then do the same as before.

5   Remember rational numbers are fractions – what do you get if you add two fractions?

6   Try 2 and √3.

7   Think what you were doing in section 4!

8   Try multiplying any old irrationals.

9   Same approach as for c).

10 Look at irrationals that are just the square root of something, and also at ones like 2 + √3.

11 Remember they are fractions!

Answers on page 89

Accuracy in calculations and dimensions

15 minutes

Test your knowledge

1
a) If $w = 4.3$ and $x = 7.6$ to one decimal place, and $y = 5$ to the nearest integer, find the upper and lower bounds of w, x and y.

b) Hence find the upper and lower bounds of the following calculations:

   i) $w + x$ ii) $wx - y$ iii) $x^2 - 3y$ iv) $\dfrac{4wx - y}{y^2}$.

2 The diagram shows triangle ABC, where the edges AB and BC are measured to the nearest centimetre.

a) Calculate the upper and lower bounds for the area of the triangle ABC.

b) Calculate the greatest error if you state the area of triangle ABC is 12 cm^2.

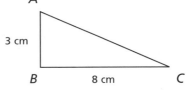

3 The letters of the alphabet are lengths. Numbers and π have no dimensions. State which of the following expressions represent a length, area, volume, or is meaningless.

a) $\pi r^2 h$ b) $a^2 + b$ c) $36\pi a$

d) $\dfrac{1}{3}(dh + bc)$ e) $\dfrac{4}{3}\pi ab$ f) $\dfrac{ab + c^2}{5}$.

✓ *If you got them all right, skip to page 24*

Accuracy in calculation and dimensions

20 minutes

Improve your knowledge

1 Measurements are never exact. They can be only be expressed to a certain degree of accuracy. When values are quoted, say to the nearest centimetre, there is a **highest** and a **lowest** value they could actually be.

The highest value is called the **upper bound**, the lowest value the **lower bound**.

Example 1 Jonathan's height was measured as 176 cm to the **nearest centimetre**.

    a) What is the tallest Jonathan could be?

    b) What is the shortest Jonathan could be?

Solution

Step 1	Halve the units	Half of 1 centimetre = 0.5 cm
Step 2	Add this to the original for the upper bound.	176 + 0.5 = 176.5 cm
	Take this away from the original for the smallest	176 − 0.5 = 175.5 cm

Jonathan's height can lie anywhere in between 175.5 cm and 176.5 cm.

Example 2 Stuart ran 400 metres in 54.3 seconds to the nearest 0.1 seconds. What is the least time he could have taken?

Solution Time in this case is measured correct to the nearest 0.1 seconds.

Step 1	Halve	0.1/2 = 0.05
Step 2	Take away	54.3 − 0.05 = 54.25 seconds.

Example 3 Phil the news reader reports that the population of the United Kingdom is 54 million, correct to the nearest million. Between what values can the real population of the UK lie?

Solution

Step 1

$$\text{Nearest million} \Rightarrow \frac{1\,000\,000}{2} = 500\,000$$

Step 2 Upper bound = 54 000 000 + 500 000 = 54 500 000
Lower bound = 54 000 000 − 500 000 = 53 500 000.
The real population can be between 53 500 000 and 54 500 000

2 Some exam questions may ask you to **calculate** the upper or lower bounds when measurements are added, subtracted, multiplied or divided.

When adding	UB = largest + largest	LB = smallest + smallest
When multipying	UB = largest × largest	LB = smallest × smallest
When subtracting	UB = largest − smallest	LB = smallest − largest
When dividing	$UB = \dfrac{\text{largest}}{\text{smallest}}$	$LB = \dfrac{\text{smallest}}{\text{largest}}$

Example 4 Given that $w = 2.7$ (to 1 d.p.), $x = 3$ (nearest whole number) and $y = 1.42$ (to 3 s.f.), find the upper and lower bounds for the following calculations:

a) $x + y$

b) $x - w$

c) wxy

d) $\dfrac{x}{wy}$.

Solution First we need to find the upper and lower bounds for each of the letters given.

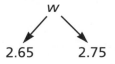   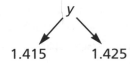

Using the table above to help us we can answer the question.

a) UB = 3.5 + 1.425 = 4.925

   LB = 2.5 + 1.415 = 3.915

b) UB = 3.5 − 2.65 = 0.85

   LB = 2.5 − 2.75 = −0.25

c) UB = 2.75 × 3.5 × 1.425 = 13.715625

   LB = 2.65 × 2.5 × 1.415 = 9.374375

d) UB = $\dfrac{3.5}{2.65 \times 1.415}$ = 0.933396 ...

   LB = $\dfrac{2.5}{2.75 \times 1.425}$ = 0.637959 ... .

Example 5 The length and width of the rectangle shown are measured to the nearest centimetre.

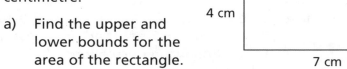

a) Find the upper and lower bounds for the area of the rectangle.

Jyoti says the area of the rectangle has got be 28 cm².

b) Calculate the maximum possible error Jyoti could make in calculating the area.

Solution

a) UB = 7.5 × 4.5 = 33.75 cm² and LB = 6.5 × 3.5 = 22.75 cm²

b) UB error = 33.75 − 28 = 5.75 cm²

   LB error = 28 − 22.75 = 5.25 cm²

The UB error is the largest $\Rightarrow$ maximum possible error = 5.75 cm².

3 **Dimensions** questions ask you to check a formula to see whether it's a formula for length, area, volume, or is meaningless.

In these questions, numbers (**and that includes** π) have no dimensions – that means they don't affect what sort of formula it is. In all these questions, the first thing you do is **cross out the numbers and** π.

All the other letters (like a, b, x, y, etc.) stand for lengths.

If a formula is for a **length**, it will only have one dimension.

Example 6   a) $2L \Rightarrow \cancel{2}L$ Length

                    b) $2\pi r \Rightarrow \cancel{2}\cancel{\pi}r$ Length

If a formula is for an **area**, it will have two dimensions, which will be either two different letters multiplied together, or one letter squared.

Example 7   a) $\pi ab \Rightarrow \cancel{\pi}ab$ Length × length, so = area

                    b) $2\pi x^2 \Rightarrow \cancel{2}\cancel{\pi}x^2$ (Length)^2, so = area

If a formula is for a **volume**, it will have three dimensions. These could be a letter cubed, three different letters multiplied together, or one letter squared multiplied by another letter.

Example 8   a) xyz Length × length × length, so = volume

                    b) $6c^2d \Rightarrow \cancel{6}c^2d$ Length^2 × length, so = volume

We can add or take away formulae of the **same** dimension.

              E.g.   'Area + area = area' or 'volume + volume = volume'.

But if we add or take away formulae of different dimensions, the answer is **rubbish!**

Example 9

a) $\pi x^2 + 2xy$
     $\cancel{\pi}x^2 + \cancel{2}xy$
     Area + area which gives area.

b) $\pi(cd + h)$
     $\cancel{\pi}(cd + h)$
     Area + length which gives rubbish!

c) $2a^2b + 17\pi efg$
     $\cancel{2}a^2b + \cancel{17}\cancel{\pi}efg$
     Volume + volume, which gives volume.

Now learn how to use your knowledge

Accuracy in calculations and dimensions

20 minutes

Use the π key on your calculator to answer this question

1 The volume of lemonade in a cylindrical drinks can is 330 cm³, measured correct to the nearest 3 cm³. The diameter of the can is 6.1 cm, correct to the nearest mm.

330 cm³

6.1 cm

Assuming that the can is **full** of lemonade:

a) State the upper and lower bounds for the volume of the can.

Hints 1–3

b) Calculate the upper and lower bounds for the height of the can.

Hints 4–9

c) Using the volume and diameter given, Elaine calculated the height of the cylinder as 11.2918…cm. Calculate the maximum possible error Elaine could make when calculating the height.

Hints 10–11

2 State the three expressions which represent an area. All the letters represent lengths.

Hints 12–13

$$\frac{1}{2}\pi r^2 \qquad abc \qquad \frac{2ab}{c} \qquad \pi ab(c + d)$$

$$\frac{4}{5}x(3y + z) \qquad wx + 5y \qquad \frac{5}{6}\pi ab \qquad 2a.$$

Hints follow

Accuracy in calculations and dimensions

Hints

1   Halve the accuracy of 3 cm³.   *1.5cm for each.*

2   Add this to the original for the UB.

3   Subtract from the original for the LB.

4   Find the UB and LB of the diameter.

5   To the nearest mm is the same as to one d.p. in this question.

6   Use volume = $\pi r^2 h$ and $d = 2r$.

7   Substitute $r = d/2$ and re-arrange the formula to make h the subject.

8   For the UB of h, the highest values go on top of the dividing line and the lowest values go underneath. Leave the 4 and π alone.

9   For the LB of h, the lowest values go on top of the dividing line and the highest values go underneath. Leave the 4 and π alone.

10 Work out the UB error and the LB error, using the values calculated in part b.

11 The largest of your two answers is the maximum possible error.

12 Cross out all the numbers and π.

13 How many dimensions in area?

Answers on page 89

Speed, distance and time

15 minutes

1 a) Dean drives 180 miles in $2\frac{1}{2}$ hours. Calculate his speed in miles per hour.

   b) Rebecca runs at 6 m/s for $1\frac{1}{2}$ minutes. How many metres has she run?

2 a) Shewley leaves her house to go to the shop. She walks 130 metres in 1 minute 40 seconds and then jogs the remaining 70 metres at 3.5 m/s. She spends 1 minute in the shop, and then runs home at 5 m/s.

   i) Draw a distance–time graph to show Shewley's journey.

   ii) At what speed did she first set out?

   iii) What is her average speed for the entire journey?

3 The graph shows the speed of an object thrown downwards into a liquid. Find the distance travelled in 0.2 seconds.

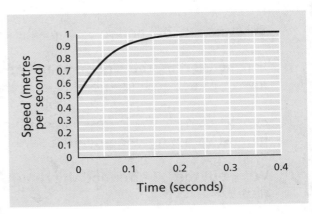

Answers

Fig. 1

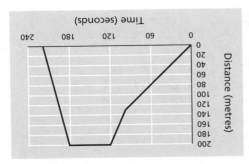

3 0.172 m
2 a) i) See Fig. 1 ii) 1.3 m/s iii) 1.82 m/s
1 a) 72 mph b) 540 m

If you got them all right, skip to page 32

Speed, distance and time

Improve your knowledge

1 You need to know the following **formulae**:

$$\text{Speed} = \frac{\text{distance}}{\text{time}} \qquad \text{Time} = \frac{\text{distance}}{\text{speed}} \qquad \text{Distance} = \text{speed} \times \text{time}$$

$$\text{Average speed} = \frac{\text{total distance}}{\text{total time}}$$

Example 1 Lychelle travels for 20 minutes at 60 km/h. How far does she travel?

Solution Distance = speed × time. But before we use the formula, we must check the units. The speed is in km/h and the time is in minutes – so we need to convert before using the formula.

Always check the units!

60 km/h is the same as 60 ÷ 60 = 1 km/minute

So distance = 1 × 20 = 20 km.

If you're not sure whether to multiply or divide by 60 remember you must travel a smaller distance in a minute than you do in an hour.

2 A **distance–time graph** has distance on the *y*-axis and time on the *x*-axis.

For a distance–time graph:

- Speed is the **gradient** of the graph. If it is a **straight–line** graph, find the gradient in the normal way.
  If it is a **curve**, draw a **tangent** and find the gradient of the tangent.

- A **positive** gradient (or speed) means you are moving **away** from the starting point; a **negative** gradient (or speed) means you are moving **towards** it.

- If there is a **horizontal** line, it means that you are **not moving**.
- You find distances and times from reading off the y- and x-axes.

Example 2   Sally sets off on her horse to visit her friend Andy. She rides at 2 m/s for 10 minutes, then 3 m/s for 5 minutes. She then stops for 5 minutes to go to a shop. She then travels the remaining 240 m to Andy's house in 8 minutes at a constant speed. Since she finds Andy is not in, she only stays at his house for 10 minutes, then returns home at a constant speed in 20 minutes.

a)   Draw a distance-time graph for Sally's journey.

b)   Find her speed on the way home.

c)   Find her average speed over the entire journey.

Solution   We have to work out what distance Sally has covered at each time in order to plot the graph: use $D = S \times T$.

But we must convert units, since speeds are in m/s and times are in minutes:

First 10 mins = $10 \times 60 = 600$ seconds, Sally travels $600 \times 2 = 1200$ metres.

Next 5 mins = $5 \times 60 = 300$ seconds, Sally travels $300 \times 3 = 900$ metres – so she's 2100 metres away after 15 mins.

Next 5 mins she does not travel, so the distance stays the same, so she's 2100 metres away after 20 mins.

Next 8 mins she travels 240 m, so she's 2340 metres away from home after 28 mins.

She stays at Andy's house for 10 minutes, so her distance stays the same, so she's 2340 metres away after 38 mins.

Next 20 minutes, she goes back home – so she travels 2340 metres in the **negative** direction

– so she's 0 metres away after 58 mins.

a) So we have this distance–time graph:

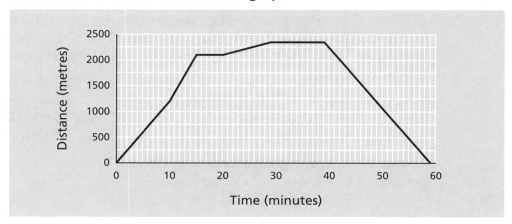

b) Speed on way home = distance ÷ time = 2340 ÷ (20 × 60) (we need time in seconds to get speed in m/s).

So speed = 1.95 m/s on way home.

c) Average speed = total distance ÷ total time.

Total distance = 2340 × 2 = 4680 metres total time = 58 mins = 3480 seconds.

So average speed = 4680 ÷ 3480 = 1.34 m/s.

Example 3 The diagram below shows how the height of a ball varies after it is thrown.

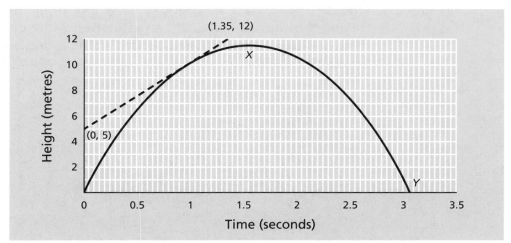

a) Describe what is happening to the ball at points *X* and *Y*.

b) Find an approximate value for the ball's speed 1 second after it has been thrown.

Solution

a) At point X, the curve has zero gradient since the tangent would be horizontal. So the ball is not moving at that point. This is when it has reached its highest point. At point Y, the ball has returned to the ground.

b) We must draw a tangent at the point when $x = 1$ and find its gradient (see diagram on page 29).

> *A tangent just* **touches** *the curve.*

To find its gradient, choose two points on it:
gradient = difference in y ÷ difference in x
= $(12 - 5) ÷ (1.35 - 0) = 5.2$ m/s.

3 A **speed–time** graph has speed on the y-axis and time on the x-axis.

For a speed–time graph:

- Distance is the **area between the graph and the x-axis**.
- A **positive** gradient means the speed is **increasing**; a **negative** gradient means the speed is **decreasing**.
- A **horizontal** line means the speed is **constant** (but you are **still** moving **unless** the speed is **zero!**).
- You find speeds and times from reading off the y- and x-axes.

Example 4 The diagram shows the speed–time graph for an object falling through a liquid. Find an estimate for the distance it has fallen in 1 second, and hence find its average speed in the first second.

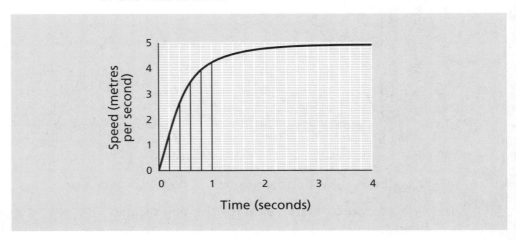

Solution   The best way to find the area under a curve is to divide it up into trapeziums and use **the trapezium rule**. This is much quicker than working out the area of all the trapeziums separately!

Step 1	Divide the area you need into trapeziums of equal width.	This is shown on the diagram – they have width 0.2
Step 2	Write down the y-values at the ends of the trapeziums.	0, 1.6, 2.6, 3.4, 3.85, 4.1
Step 3	Add up all the values **except the first and the last**.	$1.6 + 2.6 + 3.4 + 3.85 = 11.45$
Step 4	Double your answer	$11.45 \times 2 = 22.9$
Step 5	Add on the first and last values.	$22.9 + 0 + 4.1 = 27$
Step 6	Multiply by the width of the trapeziums and divide by 2.	$27 \times 0.2 \div 2 = 2.7$ m

$\therefore$ Distance fallen in 1 second is 2.7 m

Since it has fallen 2.7 m in 1 second, its average speed is $2.7 \div 1 = 2.7$ m/s.

Now learn how to use your knowledge

Speed, distance and time

1 The diagram shown is a distance–time graph for an object thrown vertically upwards from the edge of a cliff

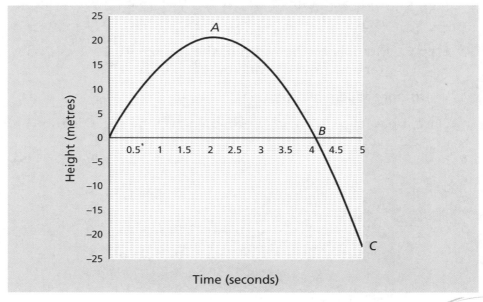

Time (seconds)

a) Estimate the speed of the object 1 second after it was thrown.

Hints 1–2

b) What is the speed at point *A*?

Hints 3–4

c) Find the highest distance above the cliff reached by the object.

Hint 5

d) Explain what is happening in the part of the graph between point *B* and point *C*.

Hints 6–7

e) What is the total distance travelled by the object in the 5 seconds?

Hint 8

✓ *Hints follow*

Speed, distance and time

1 Draw a tangent.

2 Remember to use the scale on the graph.

3 Draw a tangent at point *A* if you're not sure!

4 What does a horizontal line tell you – what gradient does it have?

5 Look on the graph to find the largest value of height.

6 The height's negative – what does that tell you?

7 Remember the height is measured from the **top** of the cliff.

8 Remember it travels up to its highest point, down to where it started then down again.

Answers on page 89

Circle theorems

Test your knowledge

1 a) Find the following angles, giving reasons for your answers:

    i) ∠BAC   ii) ∠ABC

    iii) ∠BCA.

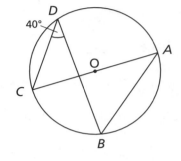

b) Find the following angles, giving reasons for your answers:

    i) ∠BCE   ii) ∠AOB

    iii) ∠BOC   iv) ∠BDC.

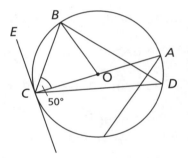

c) Find the following angles, giving reasons for your answers:

    i) ∠ADF   ii) ∠AEF

    iii) ∠CBA   iv) ∠BCD

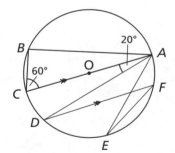

Answers

1 a) i) 40° (angles in same segment) ii) 90° (angle in a semicircle) iii) 50° (angles in a triangle sum to 180°) b) i) 40° (angle between tangent and radius = 90°) ii) 100° (angle at centre = twice angle at circumference) iii) 80° (angles on straight line sum to 180°) iv) 40° (angle at centre = twice angle at circumference) c) i) 20° (alternate angles) ii) 20° (angles in same segment) iii) 90° (angle in semicircle) iv) ∠BAC = 30° (angles in triangle) so ∠BAD = 50° so ∠BCD = 130° (opposite angles in cyclic quadrilateral)

 If you got them all right, skip to page 39

Circle theorems

Improve your knowledge

30 minutes

1 You need to learn the circle theorems given below.

Most commonly used theorems:

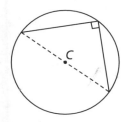

The **diameter** subtends a **right-angle**.

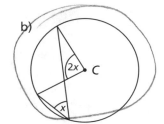

Angles subtended by the **same chord** in the **same segment** are **equal**.

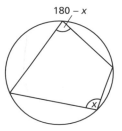

In a **cyclic** quadrilateral, **opposite** angles sum up to **180°**.

a)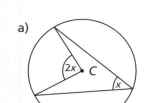

b)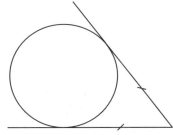

c)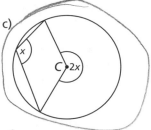

Angle at the **centre** is equal to **twice** the **angle** at the **circumference** (NB: the angles must always open out the same way as each other).

Theorems to use when there's a tangent:

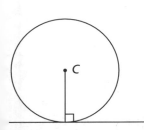

The **tangent** at a point is at **right angles** to the **radius**.

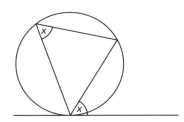

The **two tangents** from a point to a circle are **equal**.

The **angle** between a **tangent** and a **chord** is **equal** to the **angle** subtended by the **chord** in the **alternate segment**.

35

In addition to using the theorems themselves, you may also have to use any of the following rules from Intermediate work when tackling a problem:

General rules and methods

- Vertically opposite angles are equal.
- Angles in a triangle sum to 180°.
- Angles on a straight line sum to 180°.
- Recognising and using isosceles/equilateral triangles.

Rules to use with parallel lines

- Alternate angles (or Z angles) are equal.
- Corresponding angles (or F angles) are equal.
- Internal or supplementary angles sum to 180°.

Questions often ask you to **give a reason** why angles are a particular size. Although you don't have to write out the appropriate theorem in full, you do need to refer to it recognizably. 'Angle between tangent and radius' is OK, since it is obvious what you mean; 'angle with parallel line' is not, because you could be referring to any of the parallel line rules.

Here are a few strategies for dealing with circle theorems questions:

- Use the angle(s) you know, and write in any others you can work out from them
- Look at the diagram to see what you've got. If there's a tangent, you'll be using one or more of the tangent theorems; if there's a marked pair of parallel lines, you'll be using parallel line facts; if there's a cyclic quadrilateral, you'll be using that; if there's an angle at the centre, can you find one at the circumference to go with it?
- It may make it easier to see angles from the same chord/angles at centre and circumference if you draw the chord in (lightly, in pencil, so you can rub it out quickly if it is in the way).
- Don't make assumptions! Just because lines look parallel, or angles look equal, or like a right angle, doesn't mean you can **assume** they are (although if you can **prove** they are – great!).
- Use common sense as a check: if an angle looks obtuse, you should worry if you've calculated it as 30°!
- Be careful to make sure the theorems really apply. A cyclic quadrilateral must have all four corners on the circumference; the angles at the centre and circumference must 'face the same way' and be from the same chord.

Example 1 In the diagram, O is the centre of the circle and T is a tangent to the circle at B. Find angles x and y, giving reasons for your answers.

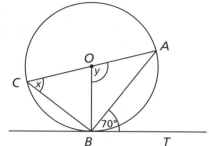

Solution Since we have a tangent, we definitely need to use one of the tangent theorems. Since we have only one tangent, it can only be alternate segment or angle between radius and tangent. Try angle between radius and tangent first (because it looks easier).

So ∠OBA = 20° because ∠OBT = 90° (angle between radius and tangent) and ∠ABT = 70°.

But △ABO is isosceles, since OA and OB are both the radius, and so are equal. So ∠OAB = 20° also.

So we have: $y = 180 - 20 - 20 = 140°$, using △OAB (angles in a triangle).

But y is an angle at the centre – so we should see if we can find the appropriate angle at the circumference.

Since both x and y are from chord AB, the angle at circumference that 'goes with' y is x.

So $x = y \div 2 = 70°$ (angle at centre = twice angle at circumference).

NB: This is not the only way we could have done the problem! You can also use the alternate segment theorem and angle subtended by a diameter. Try it!

Example 2 In the diagram below, find angles:

      a) ∠BCD   b) ∠CDF

      c) ∠ABC   d) ∠BED.

Solution Since we have a cyclic quadrilateral, we'll be using that theorem.

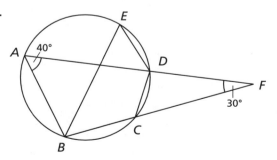

a) $\angle BCD = 180° - 40° = 140°$ since $ABCD$ is a cyclic quadrilateral.

b) This angle is not inside the circle so we have to find out something about the triangle in order to find it. We already know $\angle DFC = 30°$. From a), $\angle DCF = 180 - 140 = 40°$ (angles in a straight line) so $\angle FDC = 180° - 30° - 40° = 110°$ (angles in a triangle).

c) Since this angle is in the cyclic quadrilateral again, we can try that theorem. $\angle ABC$ is opposite $\angle ADC$ so if we can find $\angle ADC$ we can find $\angle ABC$.

But $\angle ADC = 180° - \angle FDC = 180° - 110° = 70°$ (angles in a straight line).

So $\angle ABC = 180° - \angle ADC = 180° - 70° = 110°$ (opposite angles in a cyclic quadrilateral).

d) $\angle BED$ and $\angle BAD$ are angles in the same segment and so are equal – so $\angle BED = 40°$ (or you could use the fact $BEDC$ is also a cyclic quadrilateral).

Example 3 a) Find

      i) $\angle ACD$

      ii) $\angle BEC$

    b) Show $\angle EBA$ is double $\angle DCE$.

Solution We have parallel lines, so will be using parallel line rules.

a) i) $\angle ACD = 30°$ ($\angle ACD$ and $\angle BAC$ are alternate angles).

   ii) $\angle BEC$ is an angle in the same segment as $\angle BAC$ (drawing in line makes this clearer) so $\angle BEC = 30°$ also.

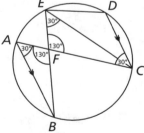

b) The easiest way to do this is to find both angles! Start by marking in what we know, and can work out easily: $\angle AFB = 130°$ (since $\angle AFB$ and $\angle EFC$ are opposite) so $\angle EBA = 180° - 130° - 30° = 20°$ (angles $\triangle ABF$) $\angle ACE = 180° - 30° - 130° = 20°$ (angles in $\triangle CEF$). We know $\angle ACD = 30°$ and $\angle ACE + \angle DCE = \angle ACD$ so $\angle DCE = 30° - 20° = 10°$ so $\angle ACE = 2 \times \angle DCE$.

Circle theorems

Use your knowledge

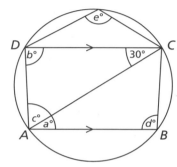

1 In the diagram below, *AC* is a diameter.

a) Find the size of all lettered angles, giving reasons for your answers in each case.

Hints 1–5

b) State what you can conclude about the quadrilateral *ABCD*.

Hints 6–7

2

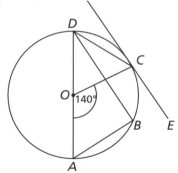

a) Explain why ∠*CBA* = 110°

Hints 8–9

b) Find ∠*DBC*, giving a reason for your answer.

Hints 10–11

c) △*BCD* is isosceles. Find:
   i) ∠*BDC* ii) ∠*BCD*.

d) Find ∠*DAB*, giving a reason for your answer.

Hint 12

e) Find ∠*ECB*, giving a reason for your answer.

Hints 13–14

Hints follow

Circle theorems

1 Use the parallel lines for *a*.

2 *a* is alternate to something. *a is alternate to* ~~turn~~ *replacement.*

3 Remember *AC* is a diameter for *b* and *d*.

4 Use the angle sum in a triangle to find *c*.

5 *e* is in a cyclic quadrilateral. Find it!

6 You can work out all its angles.

7 What sort of quadrilateral has those angles?

8 Find reflex angle $\angle AOC$.

9 You have an angle at the centre.

10 Find $\angle DBA$, and subtract.

11 Remember what line *DOA* is!

12 Cyclic quadrilateral!

13 There are only 2 tangent theorems useful here – which one applies?

14 Use the alternate segment theorem – find an angle you know from chord CB.

Answers on page 89

Trigonometry

Test your knowledge

1 For the following triangles find:

a) The lengths or angles denoted by letters

b) The area of the triangles.

i)

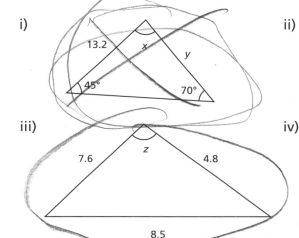

ii)

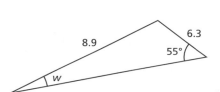

iii)

iv)

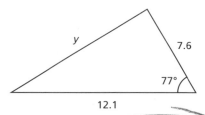

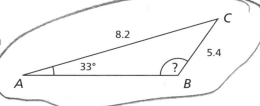

2 Find the value of the angle *ABC*, given that this angle is obtuse.

3 a) Sketch the graph of $y = -\sin x$ for $0° \leqslant x \leqslant 360°$.

b) Use your sketch in part a) to solve the equation $-\sin x = -\frac{1}{2}$ for $0° \leqslant x \leqslant 360°$.

$$2x +$$
$$x^2 + -6^x + 8 = 0$$

Answers

1 a) and b) i) $x = 65°$, $y = 9.93$ area = 59.4
(units)^2 ii) $w = 35.4°$ area = 28.0 (units)^2
iii) $z = 83.3°$ area = 18.1 (units)^2
iv) $y = 12.8$ area = 44.8 (units)^2
2 Angle = 124.2° **3** a) Graph is the result of
reflecting $y = \sin x$ in the x-axis b) $x = 30°$, 150°

✓ *If you got them all right, skip to page 47*

Trigonometry

1 By now you should know how to do right-angled trigonometry problems. This topic is covered in the Intermediate level of *GCSE Maths in a week*.

Here we look at trigonometry problems for triangles with no right angles. To do this we need to know the **sine rule** and **cosine rule**.

When doing trigonometry problems it is important to label the triangle correctly. In triangle *ABC*:

● The edge opposite angle *A* is *a*.

● The edge opposite angle *B* is *b*.

● The edge opposite angle *C* is *c*.

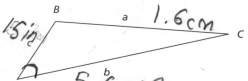

2 For the triangle *ABC* the **sine rule** says:

Either: $\dfrac{\sin A}{a} = \dfrac{\sin B}{b} = \dfrac{\sin C}{c}$ ① or $\dfrac{a}{\sin A} = \dfrac{b}{\sin B} = \dfrac{c}{\sin C}$ ②

We use formula ① when finding an angle, and formula ② when finding the length of a side.

Example 1 Find angle *x*.

Solution The angle *x* has matching edge of 8.5.

The angle 135° has matching edge of 14.

We are looking for an angle ⟹ formula ①

So $\dfrac{\sin x}{8.5} = \dfrac{\sin 135}{14}$

So $\sin x = \dfrac{\sin 135}{14} \times 8.5 = 0.42931...$

$x = \sin^{-1}(0.42931...) = 25.4°$ (3 s.f.)

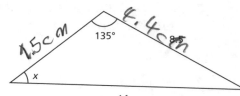

42

Example 2 Find the value of length w.

Solution

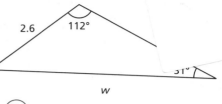

The edge w has matching angle of $112°$.

The edge 2.6 has matching angle of $31°$.

We are looking for an edge so use formula ②

$$\frac{w}{\sin 112} = \frac{2.6}{\sin 31}$$

So

$$w = \frac{2.6}{\sin 31} \times \sin 112 = 4.6806...$$

$$w = 4.68 \ (3 \ \text{s.f.})$$

An **obtuse angle** is a special case. If we use the sine rule to find an obtuse angle (any angle between $90°$ and $180°$!) we must subtract the answer we get from $180°$.

Example 3 Find the size of angle x.

Solution We are looking for an angle, so use formula ①

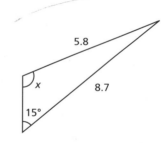

$$\Rightarrow \frac{\sin x}{8.7} = \frac{\sin 15}{5.8}$$

So

$$\sin x = \frac{\sin 15}{5.8} \times 8.7 = 0.38822...$$

$$x = \sin^{-1}(0.38822...) = 22.844...°$$

This is **too small**! The angle we are looking for is an obtuse angle, so the real value of the angle is:

$$180 - 22.844... = 157.155... \Rightarrow x = 157° \ (3 \ \text{s.f.})$$

We use the **cosine rule** when we know:

- All three edges and we want to find an angle.
- Two edges and the angle between them and we want to find the third edge.

For triangle *ABC* below the cosine rule says:

$$\cos A = \frac{b^2 + c^2 - a^2}{2bc}$$ when we are looking for an angle

$$a^2 = b^2 + c^2 - 2bc \cos A$$ when we are looking for an edge

If we have a triangle where we know the value of two edges and the angle between them (as shown opposite), then the area of the triangle is given by the formula:

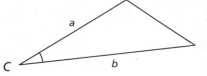

$$\text{Area of triangle} = \tfrac{1}{2} ab \sin C$$

Example 4

a) Find the area of the triangle *ABC*.

b) Find the value of *y*.

Solution

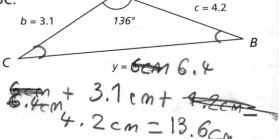

a) Area $= \tfrac{1}{2} bc \sin A$

$= \tfrac{1}{2}(3.1)(4.2)\sin 136$

$= 4.5222... = 4.52$ (3 s.f.)

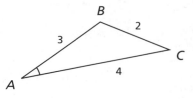

b) Using the cosine rule $y^2 = 3.1^2 + 4.2^2 - 2(3.1)(4.2)\cos 136 = 45.9816...$

So $y = \sqrt{45.9816...} = 6.78097... = 6.78$ (3 s.f.)

Example 5   Find the angle *BÂC*.

Solution We know all three edges so use cosine rule.

$$\cos A = \frac{3^2 + 4^2 - 2^2}{2 \times 3 \times 4} = 0.875$$

$A = \cos^{-1}(0.875) = 28.9550... = 29.0°$ (3 s.f.)

3 You should learn and know **how to plot the graphs of the trigonometric functions** $y = \sin x$ and $y = \cos x$, between $x = 0°$ and $x = 360°$.

- $y = \sin x°$ (Put the x-values in your calculator to get out values for sin x.)

x	0	30	60	90	120	150	180	210	240	270	300	330	360
Sin x	0	0.5	0.866	1	0.866	0.5	0	−0.5	−0.866	−1	−0.866	−0.5	0

- $y = \cos x$

x	0	30	60	90	120	150	180	210	240	270	300	330	360
Cos x	1	0.866	0.5	0	−0.5	−0.866	−1	−0.866	−0.5	0	0.5	0.866	1

The graphs of $y = \sin x$ and $y = \cos x$ are plotted below on the same axis.

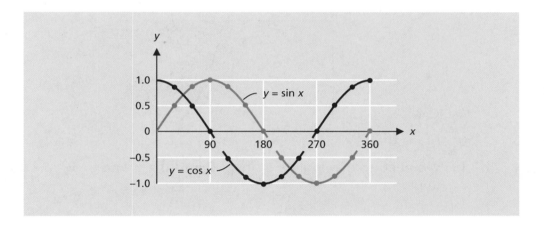

The sine graph is symmetrical about $x = 90°$ for values above the x-axis and is symmetrical about $x = 270°$ for values below the x-axis.

The cosine graph is symmetrical about $x = 180°$ for values above and below the x-axis.

Example 6   a)   Sketch the graph of $y = 2 \sin x$ for $0° \leqslant x \leqslant 360°$.

b)   Use your sketch in part a) to solve the equation $4 \sin x = 2$ for $0° \leqslant x \leqslant 360°$.

Solution

a) Try out some values:

x	0	30	60	90	120	150	180	210	240	270	300	330	360
Sin x	0	1	1.732	2	1.732	1	0	−1	−1.732	−2	−1.732	−1	0

Note that this is the sine graph stretched by scale factor 2 in the direction of the *y*-axis using transformation of curves.

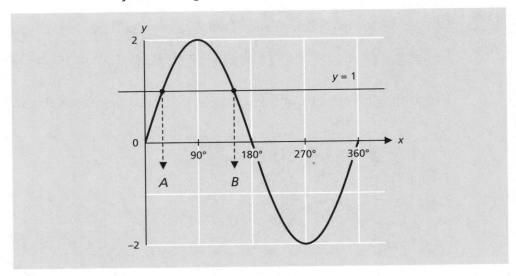

b) We need to manipulate $4 \sin x = 2$ into the graph $y = 2 \sin x$ drawn in part a).

Now $2(2 \sin x) = 2 \Longrightarrow 2 \sin x = \frac{2}{2}$.

So $2 \sin x = 1$.

We need to know the *x* values when the 'graph = 1'.

Draw line $y = 1$ on your graph for the solutions.

The line $y = 1$ cuts the graph twice, giving the *x*-solutions *A* and *B*.

To find solution *A*:

$$4 \sin x = 2 \Longrightarrow \sin x = \frac{2}{4} \Longrightarrow x = \sin^{-1}(\tfrac{1}{2}) = 30°.$$

Since the graph is symmetrical about $x = 90°$, then solution $B = 180 - 30 = 150°$.

Now learn how to use your knowledge

Trigonometry

Use your knowledge

15 minutes

1 Aneel wants to estimate the height *AC* of a tree. Aneel starts at the point *B* and finds that the angle of elevation of *B* from the top of the tree *A* is 35°. Then Aneel walks 4.5 m in a straight line to the point *D* and finds that the angle of elevation of *D* from *A* is now 47°.

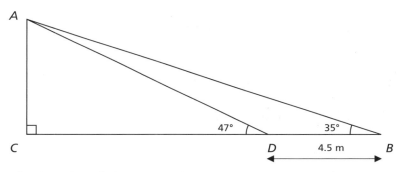

Calculate the height of the tree, giving your answer to three significant figures.

Hints 1–7

2 Anthony the engineer wants to work out the width of a busy parallel road. His boss Sophie gives Anthony a piece of paper containing the following sketch:

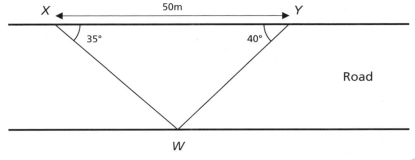

Use Sophie's sketch to calculate the width of the road, giving your answer to three significant figures.

Hints 8–12

✓ Hints follow

Trigonometry

1 Use angle AD̂C to find angle AD̂B and then angle BÂD.

2 Insert the angles in your sketch to help you to see what to do next.

3 Try to find the edge AD by using one of the trigonometry rules.

4 The edge AD has matching angle 35° and the edge 4.5 has matching angle 12°.

5 Use the sine rule to find the edge AD.

6 Use the right-angled triangle ACD and the edge AD to find AC.

7 Use the magic word 'SOHCAHTOA'.

8 Mark the width of the road on the diagram starting from W and ending at the other side of the road at Z.

9 Find the angle XŴY and mark it on the diagram.

10 The edge WY has matching angle 35° and the edge 50 m has matching angle 105°. Which rule do we use to find WY?

11 Use the edge WY, the angle 40° and the fact that WZY is a right-angled triangle.

12 Use the magic word 'SOHCAHTOA' to find the width of the road.

Answers on page 90

Areas and volumes

Test your knowledge

20 minutes

1 Find the total surface area of a closed cylinder with base radius of 6.7 cm and height 9.0 cm, giving your answer correct to 3 significant figures.

2 A cube of volume 125 cm^3 is melted down into a sphere of radius r cm, with no metal wastage. Calculate, correct to 2 significant figures, the radius of the sphere formed.

3 The diagram opposite shows the sector OXY, where the radius OY is 10 cm and the angle at the centre of the sector XOY is 56°. Calculate, correct to 3 significant figures:

a) the length of the arc XY,

b) the area of the minor segment shaded.

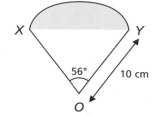

4 For the cone shown opposite, calculate:

a) the height of the cone,

b) the volume of the cone, giving your answers to 3 significant figures.

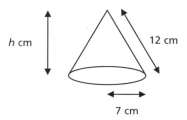

Answers

1 661 cm^2 2 3.1 cm 3 a) 9.77 cm
b) 7.42 cm^2 4 a) 9.75 cm (b) 500 cm^3

✓ *If you got them all right, skip to page 53*

49

Areas and volumes

Improve your knowledge

30 minutes

1 You need to be able to work out the lengths, areas or volumes of the shapes shown below. You need to learn the **formulae** (e) and (f) because these are not given on your formulae sheet.

a) Sphere

$V = \frac{4}{3}\pi r^3$

Surface area,
$A = 4\pi r^2$

b) Cone

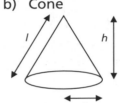

$V = \frac{1}{3}\pi r^2 h$

Curved surface area, $A = \pi r l$

c) Cylinder (closed)

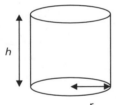

$V = \pi r^2 h$

Surface area,
$A = 2\pi r^2 + 2\pi r h$

d) Triangle

Area $= \frac{1}{2} ab \sin C$

e) Sector

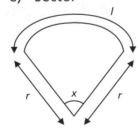

Area of sector,
$A = \dfrac{\pi r^2 x}{360}$

Length of arc,
$l = \dfrac{\pi r x}{180}$

f) Minor segment

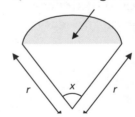

Area of minor segment,

$A = \dfrac{\pi r^2 x}{360} - \frac{1}{2} r^2 \sin x$

2 A solid metal **sphere** of radius 5 cm is melted down and formed into a **cube** of side x cm, with no wastage of metal. Calculate to 2 significant figures the value of x.

Volume of sphere, $V = \frac{4}{3}\pi r^3 = \frac{4}{3}\pi \times 5^3 = 523.5987...\text{cm}^3$

Volume of cube $= x^3 = 523.5987... \Rightarrow x = \sqrt[3]{523.5987...} = 8.05995...$

Hence $x = 8.1$ cm (2 s.f.)

3 OXY is a **sector**, with an arc length XY of 9 cm.

a) Calculate the angle x.

b) Hence calculate the area of the shaded segment shown in the diagram opposite, giving your answer correct to 2 significant figures.

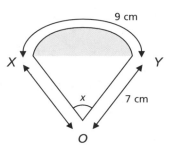

a) Length of arc, $l = \dfrac{\pi r x}{180} = 9 \Rightarrow \pi r x = 9 \times 180 \Rightarrow x = \dfrac{9 \times 180}{\pi \times r}$

Substituting values $\Rightarrow x = \dfrac{15 \times 180}{\pi \times 7} = 73.6660... \Rightarrow 73.7°$ (3 s.f.)

b) Area of minor segment $= \dfrac{\pi r^2 x}{360} - \frac{1}{2} \times r^2 \sin x$

$= \dfrac{\pi \times 7^2 \times 73.6660...}{360} - \frac{1}{2} \times 7^2 \times \sin(73.6660...)$

$= 7.98885... = 8.0$ cm^2 (2 s.f.)

4 The **cone** in figure 1 is cut along the edge OA/B and opened out to form the sector OAB, shown in figure 2, with the base circumference becoming the arc ACB. Calculate the angle, x, inside the sector as shown in figure 2, correct to 3 significant figures.

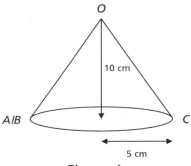

Figure 1

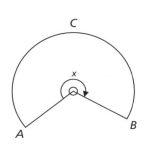

Figure 2

The idea of this question is that the area of the curved surface of the cone, in figure 1, is equal to the area inside the sector OAB.

Curved surface area $= \pi r l$, where l is the length of the slant OC.

By Pythagoras $OC = \sqrt{10^2 + 5^2} = \sqrt{125} = 11.1803....$

Hence curved surface area $= \pi \times 5 \times 11.1803... = 175.6204...cm^2$.

From Figure 2,

area of sector

$$= \frac{\pi r^2 x}{360} = 175.6204...$$

Rearranging to make x the subject gives:

$$x = \frac{175.6204... \times 360}{\pi r^2}.$$

Note radius of sector in figure 2, $r = OB = OC$, the length of the slant in figure 1.

Hence the angle

$$x = \frac{175.6204... \times 360}{\pi \times (11.1803...)^2} = 160.998... = 161° \text{ (3 s.f.)}.$$

Now learn how to use your knowledge

Areas and volumes

Use your knowledge

1 The diagram opposite shows the cross section of a cylindrical container of radius 9 cm and height 10 cm containing oil.

The greatest depth of the oil is 3 cm. Calculate:

a) the area of the shaded region.
b) the volume of the oil in the container giving your answers to 3 significant figures.

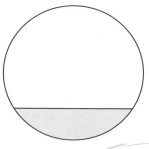

Hints 1–7

2 The diagram opposite shows a picture of Shames' toy, which consists of a cone on top of a cylinder.

Shames used his ruler to measure the lengths of some of the sides of the toy, and has included them in the diagram.

Calculate the volume of the toy giving your answer correct to 3 significant figures.

Hints 8–12

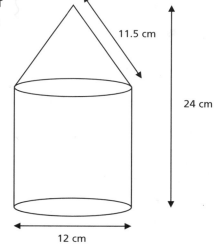

11.5 cm

24 cm

12 cm

Hints follow

Areas and volumes

1   Draw a clear and accurate diagram, joining the centre of the circle O, to both ends of the top of the oil, to form a sector.

2   Draw a vertical line from O to meet the top of the oil.

3   What is the distance from O to the top of the oil?

4   Use trigonometry to find half the angle at O using the radius and the value from Hint 3.

5   Hence find the angle at O.

6   To find the shaded region, use the formula for the area of a minor segment.

7   Use Formula Volume = (Cross Sectional Area) × (Height).

8   Work out the height of the cone by using Pythagoras' Theorem.

9   Using the height, find the volume of the cone.

10   Use the diagram to work out the height of the cylinder.

11   Hence, find the volume of the cylinder.

12   The toy consists of a cylinder and a cone.

Answers on page 90

Proportion and similar shapes

10 minutes

Test your knowledge

1 y is directly proportional to the square of x. When $x = 2$ it is known that $y = 20$.

Find:

a) The value of y when $x = 5$.

b) The value of x when $y = 31.25$.

2 W varies inversely as X. When $W = 2$ it is known that $X = 5$.

Find:

a) The value of X when $W = 4$.

b) The value of W when $X = 20$.

3 Cylinder A is similar in shape to Cylinder B.

Cylinder A has volume 5000 cm^3 and height 15 cm. Cylinder B has volume 12000 cm^3.

Calculate the height of cylinder B.

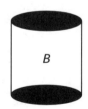

Answers

If you got them all right, skip to page 60

55

Proportion and similar shapes

Improve your knowledge

1 **Proportion** concerns two variables that are related to each other. There are two types of proportion questions that you need to know: **direct** and **inverse** proportion.

The statement '*y* is directly proportional to *x*' (written mathematically as $y \propto x$) means that when the variable *y* gets bigger, the variable *x* also gets bigger. This statement can be represented by the following graph:

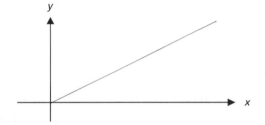

'*y* is directly proportional to *x*'

or

'*y* varies directly as *x*'

or

'*y* varies as *x*'

In maths we hate the proportional symbol $\propto$. We replace $\propto$ by ' $= k$ multiplied by', where *k* is a constant that **never** ever changes.
So '$y \propto x$' becomes '$y = kx$'.

Example 1   *y* is directly proportional to *x*. When $y = 15$, it is known that $x = 3$.

Find:

a)   The value of *y* when $x = 12$.

b)   The value of *x* when $y = 7.5$.

Solution

- Write the first statement in symbols $y \propto x$

- Get rid of the $\propto$ $y = kx$ **(1)**

- Use the given numbers to find k, the constant that never changes

  So $15 = k(3) \Rightarrow k = \dfrac{15}{3} = 5$

- Substitute the value of k into equation ① to give the magic equation

  $\boxed{y = 5x.}$

Once we have found the magic equation, we can use it to answer parts a) and b).

a) When $x = 12 \Rightarrow y = 5 \times 12 = 60$.

b) When

$$y = 7.5 \Rightarrow 7.5 = 5 \times x \Rightarrow x = \frac{7.5}{5} = 1.5.$$

There are other types of directly proportional relationships.

Example 2 Write down the following relationships using algebra and the constant k:

a) y is directly proportional to the square of x $\Rightarrow y \propto x^2 \Rightarrow y = kx^2.$

b) T varies as the square root of Q $\Rightarrow T \propto \sqrt{Q} \Rightarrow T = k\sqrt{Q}.$

2 The statement 'y is **inversely proportional** to x', (written mathematically as $y \propto 1/x$) means that when the variable y gets bigger, the variable x gets smaller. This statement can be represented by the following graph:

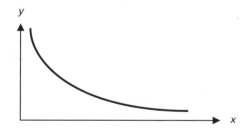

'y is inversely proportional to x'

or

'y varies inversely as x'

Again we replace $\propto$ by ' $= k$ multiplied by', where k is a constant that never changes.

So

$$y \propto \frac{1}{x}$$

becomes

$$y = k \times \frac{1}{x} \Rightarrow y = \frac{k}{x}.$$

We answer inversely proportional questions in the same way as directly proportional questions, except that 'inversely proportional' means '$\propto 1/...$'.

Example 3 C varies inversely as the square root of D.
When $C = 2$, $D = 16$.

Find:

a)   The value of C when $D = 0.5$.

b)   The value of D when $C = 4$.

- Symbols! $C \propto \dfrac{1}{\sqrt{D}}.$

- Get rid of $\propto$ $C = \dfrac{k}{\sqrt{D}}.$

- Insert numbers to find k $2 = \dfrac{k}{\sqrt{16}} \Rightarrow 2 = \dfrac{k}{4} \Rightarrow k = 8.$

- Magic equation $\boxed{C = \dfrac{8}{\sqrt{D}}.}$

a)   When

$$D = 0.5 \Rightarrow C = \frac{8}{\sqrt{0.5}} = \frac{8}{0.25} = 32.$$

b)   When

$$C = 4 \Rightarrow 4 = \frac{8}{\sqrt{D}} \Rightarrow \sqrt{D} = \frac{8}{4} = 2 \Rightarrow D = 2^2 = 4.$$

3 When faced with **similar shapes** questions you must remember the following formulae:

$$\boxed{L_{Big} = kL_{Small}} \quad \boxed{A_{Big} = k^2 A_{small}} \quad \boxed{V_{Big} = k^3 V_{Small}}$$

where k is the scale factor of enlargement (a constant that never changes), and L, A and V are length, area and volume respectively.

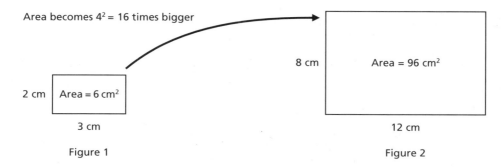

Area becomes 4^2 = 16 times bigger

8 cm | Area = 96 cm²

2 cm | Area = 6 cm²

3 cm

12 cm

Figure 1

Figure 2

Figure 1 shows a small rectangle 2 cm by 3 cm with area 6 cm².

Figure 2 shows a big rectangle which is **similar** in shape to the small rectangle. This is because the edges in the big rectangle are ($k =$) four times longer than the corresponding edges in the small rectangle. Since the edges of the small rectangle have been increased by a scale factor 4 then the area of the big rectangle is ($k^2 =$)4^2 = 16 times bigger. So i.e. $A_{Big} = 4^2 \times A_{Small} = 16 \times 6 = 96$ cm².

The same idea works for volumes of three-dimensional shapes that are similar. This means that if all the lengths of a cuboid were increased by scale factor ($k =$)3, then the volume of the new cuboid formed will be ($k^3 =$)3^3 = 27 times bigger.

Example 4   Sinneata's Soup is available in cylindrical tins of similar sizes – standard or large. The standard tin contains 290 g of soup and has diameter of 7 cm. The large tin contains 500 g of soup. Find the diameter of the large tin to one d.p.

Standard   Large

Solution

- Choose the formula where you know both quantities. We know the volume in the standard and large tin so

$V_{Big} = k^3 V_{small}$

$500 = k^3(290)$

- Insert the values to find k

So $k = \sqrt[3]{\dfrac{500}{290}} = 1.199105...$

- We want to find the diameter, which is a length, so use length formula

$L_{Big} = kL_{small} = 1.199105... \times 7$
$= 8.3937... = 8.4$ cm (1 d.p.).

✓ *Now learn how to use your knowledge*

Proportion and similar shapes

Use your knowledge

1 Suggs believes that the value of his moped £v varies inversely as the square root of its age y in years. When his moped was four years old it was valued at £1500. If this model is accurate, calculate how old the moped will be when its value falls to only £500.

Hints 1–3

2 The energy E (measured in joules) stored in an elastic band is directly proportional to the square of the extension x (measured in cm). The elastic band has been extended by 4 cm. Calculate how much **further** the elastic band must be extended for the energy stored in it to double.

Hints 4–9

3 Two similar drinking cups have heights of 12 cm and 15 cm respectively. Find:

a) The capacity of the smaller cup, if the large cup has capacity of 600 cm³.

Hints 10–12

b) The ratio of the surface area of the larger cup to the smaller cup.

Hints 13–14

✔ *Hints follow*

Proportion and similar shapes

Hints

1 Write the first sentence in symbols then get rid of the $\propto$.

2 Find k and write down the 'magic equation'.

3 Substitute $v = 500$ into the magic equation and then re-arrange to find y.

4 Write the first sentence in symbols, get rid of $\propto$.

5 Write down the energy when $x = 4$. Call this equation ①.

6 If the original energy is E then double the energy is …

7 Write down an equation for $2E$ and call this equation ②.

8 Substitute ① into ② to find x, the extension of the elastic band.

9 The question asks for the **further** extension, beyond when x was 4 cm.

10 We have both lengths so write down the length formula.

11 Insert the heights we know to find the constant k.

12 Capacity means volume so use volume formula to find the small volume.

13 The ratio of the area is found by $\dfrac{A_{BIG}}{A_{SMALL}}$

14 This is just $k^2\left(=\dfrac{A_{BIG}}{A_{SMALL}}\right)$

Answers on page 90

Vectors

Test your knowledge

1 OACB is a parallelogram where the point W is the mid-point of OA and the point X is the mid-point of BC.

The vectors $\overrightarrow{OA} = \mathbf{a}$ and $\overrightarrow{OB} = \mathbf{b}$.

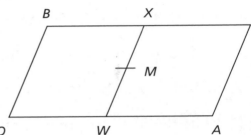

a) Find in terms of **a** and **b** the vectors:

  i) $\overrightarrow{OC}$ ii) $\overrightarrow{OW}$ iii) $\overrightarrow{OX}$

  iv) $\overrightarrow{WX}$ v) $\overrightarrow{AX}$ vi) $\overrightarrow{AB}$.

b) What can be deduced about the lines OB and WX?

c) Given that the point M is the mid-point of the line WX, find in terms of **a** and **b**, the vectors:

  i) $\overrightarrow{WM}$ ii) $\overrightarrow{OM}$ iii) $\overrightarrow{AM}$ iv) $\overrightarrow{MB}$.

d) What can be deduced about the points A, M and B?

2 A liner can sail at 13 knots in still water. The liner is sailing due South. Given that there is a current of 5 knots flowing in an easterly direction, calculate the actual speed of the liner (in knots) and its actual direction (in bearings).

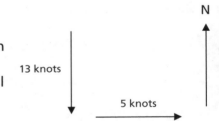

Answers

direction = 159° (nearest degree).
length. **2** Speed = 13.93... knots,
on a straight line and are of the same
iii) $-\frac{1}{2}\mathbf{a} + \mathbf{b}$ **iv)** $\frac{1}{2}\mathbf{a} + \frac{1}{2}\mathbf{b}$ **d)** The points lie
b) $\frac{1}{2}\mathbf{a} + \frac{1}{2}\mathbf{b}$ **c) i)** $\frac{1}{2}\mathbf{b}$ **ii)** $\frac{1}{2}\mathbf{a} + \frac{1}{2}\mathbf{b}$
and of the same length **c) i)** $\frac{1}{2}\mathbf{b}$ **ii)** $\frac{1}{2}\mathbf{a} + \frac{1}{2}\mathbf{b}$
v) $-\frac{1}{2}\mathbf{a} + \mathbf{b}$ **vi)** $-\mathbf{a} + \mathbf{b}$ **b)** vectors are parallel
1 a) i) $\mathbf{a} + \mathbf{b}$ **ii)** $\frac{1}{2}\mathbf{a}$ **iii)** $\frac{1}{2}\mathbf{a} + \mathbf{b}$ **iv)** $\frac{1}{2}\mathbf{a} + \mathbf{b}$ **v)** $\mathbf{b}$

 If you got them all right, skip to page 66

Vectors

1 **Scalars** (e.g. mass, length, time, speed) are quantities that have **magnitude** only. **Vectors** (e.g. velocity, acceleration, force) are quantities that have **magnitude** and **direction**. In most text books (including this one!) vectors are represented by bold letters, e.g. **a**, **x** but when you write them down it is usual to underline them, e.g. $\underline{a}$, $\underline{x}$.

Example 1 *WXYZ* is a trapezium. Given that $\vec{WX} = $ **a** $\vec{XY} = $ **b** $\vec{ZY} = 3$**a** find in terms of **a** and **b** the vectors:

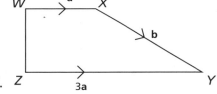

a) $\vec{YZ}$ b) $\vec{WY}$ c) $\vec{WZ}$ d) $\vec{YW}$.

Solution

a) $\vec{YZ} = -3$**a** (We are going against the arrow, so the vector 3**a** becomes negative.)

b) $\vec{WY} = \vec{WX} + \vec{XY} = $ **a** + **b** It's like a journey: to get from *W* to *Y* you first go from *W* to *X*, then from *X* to *Y*.

c) $\vec{WZ} = \vec{WX} + \vec{XY} + \vec{YZ} = $ **a** + **b** $- 3$**a** $= -2$**a** + **b**.

d) $\vec{YW} = \vec{YX} + \vec{XW} = -$**b** $-$ **a**.

Example 2 *ABCDEF* is a regular hexagon. Given that $\vec{OF} = $ **a** and $\vec{OE} = $ **b**

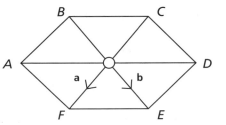

a) Find in terms of **a** and **b**, the vectors:

i) $\vec{FE}$ ii) $\vec{AD}$.

b) Hence write down the vector $\vec{BC}$.

c) What geometrical fact is exhibited by the vectors $\vec{BC}$ and $\vec{AD}$?

63

Solution

a) i) $\vec{FE} = \vec{FO} + \vec{OE} = -\mathbf{a} + \mathbf{b}$.

   ii) $\vec{AD} = \vec{AF} + \vec{FO} + \vec{OE} + \vec{ED} = \mathbf{b} - \mathbf{a} + \mathbf{b} - \mathbf{a} = -2\mathbf{a} + 2\mathbf{b}$

   ($\vec{AF}$ is the same length and direction as $\vec{OE}$. Note that $\vec{AF} = \mathbf{b}$

   $\vec{ED}$ is the same length and direction as $\vec{FO}$ so $\vec{ED} = -\mathbf{a}$.)

b) The vectors $\vec{BC}$ and $\vec{FE}$ are parallel, the same length and
   direction $\Rightarrow \vec{BC} = \vec{FE} \Rightarrow \vec{BC} = -\mathbf{a} + \mathbf{b}$.

c) $\vec{AD} = -2\mathbf{a} + 2\mathbf{b} = 2(-\mathbf{a} + \mathbf{b}) = 2\vec{BC}$
   So vector $\vec{AD}$ is twice the length and is parallel vector $\vec{BC}$.

Example 3

OWX is a triangle where *A* is
the mid-point of the line *OW*
and *B* is the mid-point of the
line *OX*. Also *N* lies on the
edge *WX* such that *WN* : *NX* is
1 : 2. Given that $\vec{OA} = \mathbf{a}$ $\vec{OB} = \mathbf{b}$

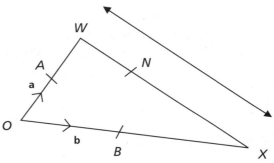

a) Find in terms of **a** and **b**, the vectors:

   i) $\vec{OW}$ ii) $\vec{OX}$ iii) $\vec{WX}$ iv) $\vec{WN}$ v) $\vec{ON}$.

b) Hence prove that the vector $\vec{AB}$ is parallel to the vector $\vec{WN}$.

Solution

a) i) $\vec{OW} = 2\vec{OA} = 2\mathbf{a}$. Because $\vec{OW}$ is in the same direction but twice
   the distance of $\vec{OA}$.

   ii) Hence $\vec{OX} = 2\vec{OB} = 2\mathbf{b}$.

   iii) $\vec{WX} = \vec{WO} + \vec{OX} = -2\mathbf{a} + 2\mathbf{b}$

   iv) Since *N* splits up the line *WX* in the ratio of 1 : 2, then
   $\vec{WN} = \frac{1}{3}\vec{WX}$.
   Hence $\vec{WN} = \frac{1}{3}(-2\mathbf{a} + 2\mathbf{b})$, using part (iii), giving $\vec{WN} = -\frac{2}{3}\mathbf{a} + \frac{2}{3}\mathbf{b}$.

   v) $\vec{ON} = \vec{OW} + \vec{WN} = 2\mathbf{a} + (-\frac{2}{3}\mathbf{a} + \frac{2}{3}\mathbf{b}) = \frac{4}{3}\mathbf{a} + \frac{2}{3}\mathbf{b}$

b) First $\vec{AB} = \vec{AO} + \vec{OB} = -\mathbf{a} + \mathbf{b}$.

   Hence $\vec{WN} = -\frac{2}{3}\mathbf{a} + \frac{2}{3}\mathbf{b} = \frac{2}{3}(-\mathbf{a} + \mathbf{b}) = \frac{2}{3}\vec{AB}$.

   So vector $\vec{WN}$ is two-thirds of the length (and in the same direction
   as) $\vec{AB}$ and hence $\vec{WN}$ is parallel to $\vec{AB}$.

2 **Speed** is a **scalar** quantity which has only a magnitude, but **velocity** is a **vector** quantity which has both a **value** and a **direction**.

Example 4

Mitch wants to swim due North across a river. There is a current of 1.2 m/s in an easterly direction across the river. Given that Mitch can swim at 0.8 m/s in still water, find:

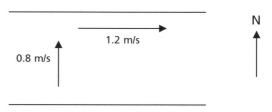

a) Mitch's actual velocity expressed as a magnitude and a direction in bearings.

b) The river is 25 m wide. Calculate the time taken for Mitch to swim across the river.

Solution

a) To find Mitch's actual velocity we must add the vectors together as shown opposite. The resultant vector **v** is Mitch's actual velocity.

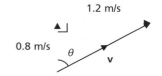

Using Pythagoras, magnitude, $v = \sqrt{0.8^2 + 1.2^2} = \sqrt{2.08} = 1.44222...$ $= 1.44$ m/s is 3 s.f.

Using trigonometry, the bearing $= \theta \Rightarrow \tan\theta = \dfrac{1.2}{0.8} \Rightarrow \theta = \tan^{-1}(1.5) = 56.3°$.

b) We use

$$\text{Speed} = \frac{\text{Distance}}{\text{Time}} \Rightarrow \text{Time} = \frac{\text{Distance}}{\text{Speed}}$$

The distance across the river is 25 m. We say speed = 0.8 m/s because this is the part of the velocity which is concerned with how fast Mitch crosses the water from one side to the other (in a northerly direction). We ignore the 1.2 m/s part of the velocity because this part will make Mitch go further downstream.

Hence time $= \dfrac{25}{0.8} = 31.25$ seconds.

Now learn how to use your knowledge

Vectors

Use your knowledge

1 The diagram opposite shows a trapezium *OABC*, where the point *R* is located on *AB* such that *AR* : *RB* = 1 : 3.

a) Given that $\overrightarrow{OA}$ = **a** $\overrightarrow{OB}$ = **b** and $\overrightarrow{BC}$ = 3**a**, find in terms of **a** and **b** the vectors:

i) $\overrightarrow{OC}$ ii) $\overrightarrow{AB}$ iii) $\overrightarrow{AC}$
iv) $\overrightarrow{OR}$ v) $\overrightarrow{RC}$.

Hints 1–8

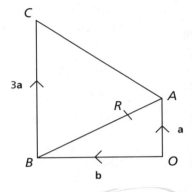

b) Prove that the vectors $\overrightarrow{OR}$ and $\overrightarrow{RC}$ are parallel.

Hints 9–10

c) What can also be deduced about the points *O*, *R* and *C*?

Hints 11–12

2 A ship can sail at 14 knots in still water. The ship is sailing in the direction of due North. There is a current of 6 knots flowing in a North-easterly direction.

a) Draw a vector diagram showing the direction in which the ship is actually heading.

Hints 13–14

b) Calculate the actual speed of the ship.

Hint 15

c) Calculate as a bearing, the direction in which the ship actually travels.

Hints 16–17

✓ *Hints follow*

Vectors

1 i) Think of vectors like a journey by planning a route using vectors you already know, i.e. $\overrightarrow{OC} = \overrightarrow{OB} + \overrightarrow{BC}$.

2 ii) Take a route via O.

3 iii) To go from AC take a route via O then B.

4 iv) First write down a route from O to R via A for example.

5 iv) Use the ratio given in the question to find the vector AR.

6 iv) AR is a quarter of the length of AB.

7 v) Plan a route using some vectors that you know.

8 v) Use the route $\overrightarrow{RC} = \overrightarrow{RO} + \overrightarrow{OC}$.

9 b) To prove vectors are parallel you need to prove one vector is a multiple of the other.

10 b) Write down $\overrightarrow{RC}$ and see how many times it is bigger than $\overrightarrow{OR}$.

11 c) Use the fact proved in part b).

12 c) Which point is common to vectors $\overrightarrow{OR}$ and $\overrightarrow{RC}$? What does this mean?

13 Join the vectors together, starting with the 14 knots vector followed by the 6 knots vector.

14 Draw an edge on the diagram from where you started to where you have finished. This edge represents the actual speed of the ship.

15 Use the cosine rule on your diagram to find the actual speed.

16 The bearing is the angle between the 14 knots vector and the actual velocity vector.

17 Use either the cosine rule or the sine rule to find the angle.

Answers on page 91

Probability and statistics

15 minutes

Test your knowledge

1. Mr Chalk is a teacher who has a pencil case with three red pens and seven black pens. He takes out two pens from it at random to take home with him every night.

   a) When Mr Chalk has a lot of marking, he needs two red pens to get through it all. What is the probability he gets the two red pens he needs?

   b) On most nights, Mr Chalk needs one pen of each colour. What is the probability that happens?

2. Draw a histogram to represent the following data on heights of some people:

Height (cm)	$150 \leqslant x < 160$	$160 \leqslant x < 165$	$165 \leqslant x < 170$	$170 \leqslant x < 175$	$175 \leqslant x < 180$	$180 \leqslant x < 200$
Frequency	4	5	12	15	10	10

3. a) Find the mean and standard deviation of 3, 7, 11, 15, and **hence** state the mean and standard deviation of:

   i) 1, 5, 9, 13   ii) 6, 14, 22, 30   iii) 26, 34, 42, 50.

   b) Find the mean and standard deviation of the data on heights from Question 2.

Answers

b) mean = 173.30 cm, S.D. = 9.73 cm
iii) mean = 38, S.D. = 8.94
i) mean = 7, S.D. = 4.47 ii) mean = 18, S.D. = 8.94
2.4 3, 2, 0.5. **3** a) mean = 9, S.D. = 4.47.
10, 5, 5, 5, 20 and frequency densities 0.4, 1,
1 a) $\frac{1}{15}$ b) $\frac{7}{30}$. **2** Plot a histogram with class widths

✓ If you got them all right, skip to page 74

68

Probability and statistics

Improve your knowledge

1 In addition to the Intermediate level work (see GCSE Maths in a week), you need to be able to draw and use more advanced **probability tree diagrams** and deal with more complicated problems. You will sometimes find that the second branch of the tree diagram depends on the first:

Example 1 Samina goes on holiday to France or Spain. The probability she goes to France is 0.2. She always goes either for one week or two weeks. If she goes to France, the probability she goes for one week is 0.6. If she goes to Spain, the probability she goes for one week is 0.3.

a) Draw a tree diagram to represent this information.

b) What is the probability Samina goes on holiday for two weeks?

Solution

a)

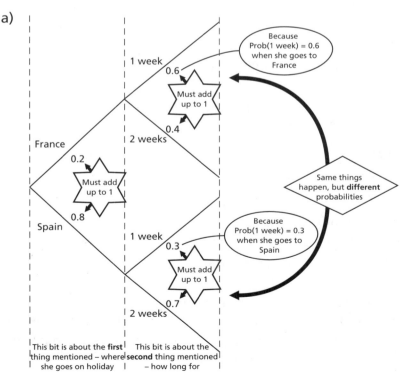

b) We want the branches 'France 2 weeks' and 'Spain 2 weeks':

P(France 2 weeks) = 0.2 × 0.4 = 0.08

P(Spain 2 weeks) = 0.8 × 0.7 = 0.56

So P(2 weeks) = 0.08 + 0.56 = 0.64.

> *Remember – multiply along branches, add different branches.*

Example 2   Andy has a bag containing 5 red sweets and 4 green sweets. He takes 2 sweets out, one at a time.

a) Find the probability they are both the same.

b) Write down the probability they are different colours.

Solution   Even though it does not tell us to draw a diagram, it is still necessary to do it!

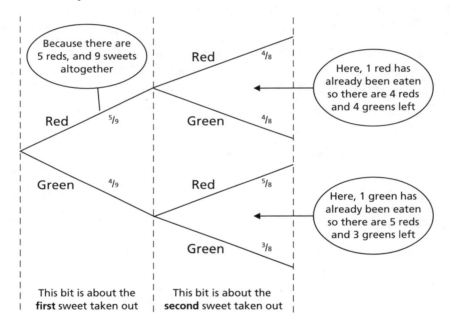

> Because there are 5 reds, and 9 sweets altogether

> Here, 1 red has already been eaten so there are 4 reds and 4 greens left

> Here, 1 green has already been eaten so there are 5 reds and 3 greens left

This bit is about the **first** sweet taken out

This bit is about the **second** sweet taken out

a) We want the branches 'Red Red' and 'Green Green':

P(Red Red) = $\frac{5}{9} \times \frac{4}{8} = \frac{5}{18}$

P(Green Green) = $\frac{4}{9} \times \frac{3}{8} = \frac{1}{6}$

So P(the same) = $\frac{5}{18} + \frac{1}{6} = \frac{4}{9}$.

b) The sweets are different if they are not the same.

So P(different) = 1 − P(the same) = $1 - \frac{4}{9} = \frac{5}{9}$.

> *This is called the 'not rule'.*

2   You may be asked to draw or use a **histogram**. Histograms are drawn from grouped frequency tables, and the **area** tells you how many people (or the **frequency**). So if an area of 3 cm² represented one person, an area of 6 cm² would represent two people.

Example 3 Draw a histogram for the following data on the weights of some small objects:

Weight (g)	$0\,g<x\leqslant10\,g$	$10\,g<x\leqslant20\,g$	$20\,g<x\leqslant25\,g$	$25\,g<x\leqslant30\,g$	$30\,g<x\leqslant50\,g$
Frequency (f)	5	10	10	15	5

Step 1 Add two columns to the table you're given, with the extra headings 'class width' and 'frequency density'.

Step 2 Fill in the class width column, by taking the lower x-value away from the higher x-value.

Step 3 Fill in the frequency density column, by using the formula: frequency density = frequency ÷ class width.

Step 4 On graph paper, mark scales for weight (x-axis) and frequency density (y-axis) (must be this way round!).

Step 5 Draw a 'box' for each class; the one for $10\,g<x\leqslant20\,g$ would go between 10 and 20 on the x-axis, and up to 1 on the y-axis.

x	f	Class width	Frequency density
$0\,g<x\leqslant10\,g$	5	$10-0=10$	$5\div10=0.5$
$10\,g<x\leqslant20\,g$	10	$20-10=10$	$10\div10=1$
$20\,g<x\leqslant25\,g$	10	$25-20=5$	$10\div5=2$
$25\,g<x\leqslant30\,g$	15	$30-25=5$	$15\div5=3$
$30\,g<x\leqslant50\,g$	5	$50-30=20$	$5\div20=0.25$

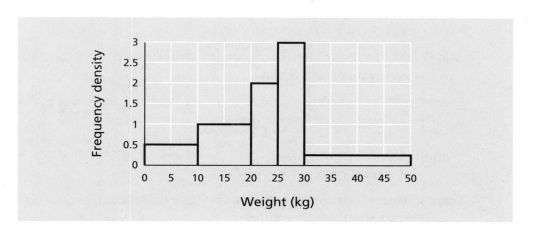

71

3 In addition to calculating mean, median, mode and interquartile range (which you should know from Intermediate work), you also have to be able to calculate the **standard deviation (SD)** of a set of numbers. Here's how:

Find the SD of 1, 2, 4, 5, 7.

Step 1	Find the mean of the numbers.	$\dfrac{1+2+4+5+7}{5} = 3.8$
Step 2	Square the mean.	$3.8^2 = 14.44$
Step 3	Square all the numbers.	$1^2 = 1 \quad 2^2 = 4 \quad 4^2 = 16$ $5^2 = 25 \quad 7^2 = 49$
Step 4	Add up the squares.	$1 + 4 + 16 + 25 + 49 = 95$
Step 5	Divide by how many there are.	$95 \div 5 = 19$
Step 6	Take the square of the mean away from your last answer.	$19 - 14.44 = 4.56$
Step 7	Square root the answer to (6).	$\sqrt{4.56} = 2.14$ (2 d.p.).

You may also have to calculate it for frequency tables. In this case we have to use a formula:

Standard deviation = $\sqrt{[(\text{sum of all } fx^2 \text{ values}) \div (\text{sum of all } f \text{ values}) - \text{mean}^2]}$.

Example 4 Find the standard deviation of the following data:

Weight (g)	$0\,g < x \leqslant 10\,g$	$10\,g < x \leqslant 20\,g$	$20\,g < x \leqslant 25\,g$	$25\,g < x \leqslant 30\,g$	$30\,g < x \leqslant 50\,g$
Frequency (f)	10	10	10	15	5

Solution

Step 1	Add three rows to the table above, with the extra headings 'Midpoint (x)' 'fx' and 'fx^2'.
Step 2	Fill in the midpoint (x) row by averaging the top and bottom weights for each class.
Step 3	Fill in the 'fx' row by doing $f \times x$, and the 'fx^2' row by $f \times x \times x$.
Step 4	Add up the f, fx and fx^2 rows.
Step 5	Work out the mean ($=$ total of $fx \div$ total of f).	Mean $= 1037.5 \div 50 = 20.75$
Step 6	Use the formula to work out standard deviation.	$SD = \sqrt{[(26906.25 \div 50) - 20.75^2]}$ $= \sqrt{(538.125 - 430.5625)} = 10.37$

What happens to the SD and mean when the **values change**?

- If all the values have the same number **added or subtracted**:
  The SD does not change.
  You add or subtract the number from the mean.

- If all the values are **multiplied or divided** by the same number:

  The SD and mean are multiplied or divided by the number.

Example 5

a) Find the mean and standard deviation of 1, 2, 3, 4, 5.

b) Write down the mean and SD of:

    i)   6, 7, 8, 9, 10

    ii) 3, 6, 9, 12, 15

    iii) 103, 106, 109, 112, 115.

c) Explain why any five consecutive integers will have the same SD as 1, 2, 3, 4, 5.

Solution

a) Mean $= \dfrac{1+2+3+4+5}{5} = 3$

To find SD: $mean^2 = 3^2 = 9$ and
$1^2 = 1 \qquad 2^2 = 4 \qquad 3^2 = 9 \qquad 4^2 = 16 \qquad 5^2 = 25$.

$\dfrac{1+4+9+16+25}{5} = 11 \qquad 11 - 9 = 2$. So SD $= \sqrt{2} = 1.41$ (2 d.p.).

b) i)   We've added 5 to all values:

      new mean $= 3 + 5 = 8$ new SD $=$ old SD $= 1.41$

  ii) We've multiplied all the values by 3:

      new mean $= 3 \times 3 = 9$ new SD $= 3 \times 1.41 = 4.23$

  iii) We've added 100 to the values in part ii):

      new mean $= 9 + 100 = 109$ new SD $= 4.23$.

c) Because we can get any other five consecutive integers by just adding numbers to 1, 2, 3, 4, 5, which leaves the standard deviation unaffected.

Now learn how to use your knowledge

Probability and statistics

20 minutes

Use your knowledge

1 I have a bag containing two yellow and six black balls. I take out three balls, one at a time.

a) What is the probability they are all the same colour? *Hints 1–3*

b) State the probability I get at least one yellow ball. *Hint 4*

c) What is the probability I get exactly one yellow ball? *Hint 5*

2 Jagjit is tossing a fair coin. He tosses it N times. The probability he gets at least one head is $\frac{31}{32}$.

a) Write down the probability he gets all tails. *Hints 6–7*

b) What is N? *Hints 8–9*

3 i) Show that the mean of $-15, -10, -5, 0, 5, 10, 15$ is 0, and find the standard deviation of these figures. *Hint 10*

ii) Hence find the mean and standard deviation of $-3, -2, -1, 0, 1, 2, 3$. *Hints 11–12*

iii) Hence find the mean and standard deviation of $-3a, -2a, -a, 0, a, 2a, 3a$. *Hint 13*

Hints follow

Probability and statistics

1 Draw a tree diagram – it needs three stages in it.

2 Don't forget the number of balls left goes down by 1 each time.

3 All the same means all black or all yellow – but all yellow is impossible.

4 P(At least one yellow) = 1 – P(no yellows).

5 There are three paths you need to use – work out the probability for each, then add them up.

6 All tails = no heads.

7 P(no heads) = 1 – P(at least one head).

8 Work out P(all tails) for different values of N until you get one that works.

9 Multiply probabilities!

10 Normal method for mean and standard deviation – but remember a negative number squared is positive!

11 What have you done to the first lot of numbers to get these?

12 You've divided by something – what is it?

13 You've multiplied by a.

Answers on page 91

Graphs

20 minutes

1 The diagram opposite shows the graph of $y = f(x)$ where $f(x) = x^2 + 2x - 15$ with the points A and B where the graph cuts the x axis and C, the minimum point on the curve.

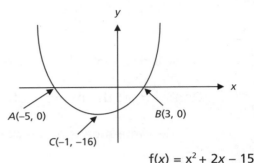

$A(-5, 0)$ $B(3, 0)$

$C(-1, -16)$

$f(x) = x^2 + 2x - 15$

Sketch on separate axis, the graphs of:

a) $y = f(2x)$ b) $y = 2f(\frac{1}{2}x)$ c) $y = -f(x - 3)$

stating the new coordinates of A, B and C for each graph.

2 The table opposite gives the values of variables x and y which are believed to be related by the law $y = Ax^2 + B$ where A and B are constants.

x	3.2	4.5	6	6.3	7
y	20	13	2.5	0	-6

By drawing a suitable graph:

a) Confirm that the law is approximately true.

b) Find the values of the constants A and B, and state the law y, in terms of x.

Answers

1 a) Graph drawn is a stretch of $f(x)$, scale factor $\frac{1}{2}$ parallel to the x axis. The new points are $A(-2.5, 0)$, $B(1.5, 0)$ and $C(-\frac{1}{2}, -16)$ b) Graph drawn is a stretch of $f(x)$, scale factor 2 parallel to both the x and y axis (i.e. an enlargement scale factor 2). The new points are $A(-10, 0)$, $B(6, 0)$ and $C(-2, -32)$. c) Graph drawn is the graph of $f(x)$ reflected in the x axis, followed by a translation of 3 units to the right. The new points are $A(-2, 0)$, $B(6, 0)$ and $C(2, 16)$

2 a) Plot a graph of y against x^2 using the points: x^2: 10.24, 20.25, 36, 39.69, 49 and y: 20, 13, 2.5, 0, -6. When plotted the scatter points lie on a straight line. Hence the law $y = Ax^2 + B$ must be true. b) The intercept $C = B \approx 27$, and the gradient $M = A \approx -0.7$ (1 s.f.). The law is approximately $y = -0.7x^2 + 27$

 If you got them all right, skip to page 82

Graphs

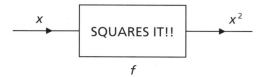

35 minutes

1 A **function** is a rule which converts *'input'* values to *'output'* values. A function usually consists of 3 components: *input*, *rule* and *output*.

Example 1 $f(x) = x^2$ is a function.

x → | SQUARES IT!! | → x^2

f

The input is a value, say x. The rule of the function is the SQUARE the input. Hence the output is x^2.

You must know the graphs of x^2, x^3, $1/x$, $\sin x$ and $\cos x$. Once you have learnt how to draw these graphs, you can use the method of **transformation of curves** to draw more complicated curves.

If you start with the basic graph of $y = f(x)$ then the graph:

- $y = f(x) + A$ moves up A units.
- $y = f(x) - A$ moves down A units.
- $y = f(x - A)$ moves to the right A units.
- $y = f(x + A)$ moves to the left A units.
- $y = f(Ax)$ stretches with scale factor 1/A parallel to the x-axis.
- $y = Af(x)$ stretches with scale factor A parallel to the y-axis.
- $y = -f(x)$ reflects in the x-axis.
- $y = f(-x)$ reflects in the y-axis.

where A is a positive number.

Example 2 The diagram shows the graph of $f(x) = x^2$.

Sketch the graphs of:

i) $y = f(x) + 3$

ii) $y = f(x - 2)$

iii) $y = f(x + 1) - 2$

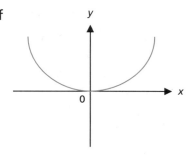

and for each graph:

a) Describe the geometrical transformation from the graph of $y = f(x)$.

b) State the minimum value and the value of x for which it occurs.

c) Write its equation y in terms of x.

i) a) Original curve has moved up 3 units (Draw same curve but at new origin of (0, 3).)

$\Rightarrow$ Translation $\begin{pmatrix} 0 \\ 3 \end{pmatrix}$

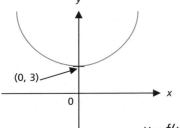

b) Minimum value $\Rightarrow$ lowest y-value on the graph $\Rightarrow y = 3$ and the value of x is $x = 0$.

$y = f(x) + 3$

c) Since $f(x) = x^2$, then $y = f(x) + 3$ becomes $y = x^2 + 3$.

ii) a) Original curve has moved to the right by 2 units

$\Rightarrow$ Translation $\begin{pmatrix} 2 \\ 0 \end{pmatrix}$

(Draw same curve, but at new origin (2, 0).)

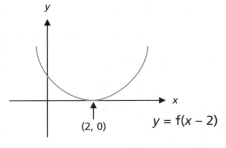

b) Minimum value $\Rightarrow$ lowest y-value on the graph $\Rightarrow y = 0$ and the value of x is $x = 2$.

$y = f(x - 2)$

c) Since $f(x) = x^2$, then $y = f(x - 2)$ becomes $y = (x - 2)^2$.

iii) a) Original curve has moved left one unit, then down by two units.

Translation $\begin{pmatrix} -1 \\ -2 \end{pmatrix}$

(Draw same curve, but at new origin (-1, -2).)

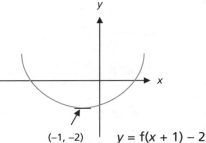

b) Minimum value is $y = -2$ and the value of x is $x = -1$.

$y = f(x + 1) - 2$

c) Since $f(x) = x^2$, then $y = f(x + 1) - 2$ becomes $y = (x + 1)^2 - 2$.

Example 3

The diagram shows a sketch of the graph $y = f(x)$ where $f(x) = -x^2 + 2x + 8$.

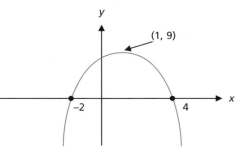

Sketch the graphs of:

a) $y = f(2x)$ b) $y = -f(x)$

c) $y = \frac{1}{2}f(\frac{1}{2}x)$

and work out the equation of the curve y, in terms of x.

a) This is the case $y = f(Ax)$ where $A = 2$. This means you stretch the curve $y = f(x)$ with scale factor $\frac{1}{2}$ parallel to the x-axis. (i.e. You halve all the x-coordinates and leave the y-coordinates alone.)

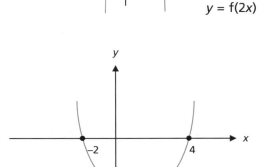

$y = f(2x) = -(2x)^2 + 2(2x) + 8$

$\Rightarrow y = -4x^2 + 4x + 8$

b) This is the case $y = -f(x)$. This means you reflect the curve $y = f(x)$ in the x-axis. (i.e. You turn the graph $y = f(x)$ upside down about the x-axis.)

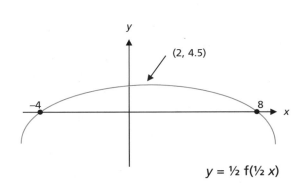

$y = -f(x) = -(-x^2 + 2x + 8)$

$\Rightarrow y = x^2 - 2x - 8$

c) This is a combination of the cases $y = f(Ax)$ where $A = \frac{1}{2}$ and $y = Af(x)$ where $A = \frac{1}{2}$.

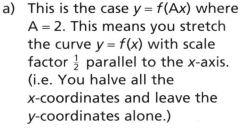

This means the curve $y = f(x)$ is stretched by a scale factor of 2 ($= 1/0.5$) parallel to the x-axis and scale factor of $\frac{1}{2}$ parallel to the y-axis.

$$y = \tfrac{1}{2} f(\tfrac{1}{2} x) = \tfrac{1}{2}(-(\tfrac{1}{2} x)^2 + 2(\tfrac{1}{2} x) + 8)$$
$$\Rightarrow y = \tfrac{1}{2}(-\tfrac{1}{4} x^2 + x + 8)$$
$$\Rightarrow y = -\tfrac{1}{8} x^2 + \tfrac{1}{2} x + 4.$$

2 When doing experiments you may believe that there is some law that exists between two sets of data, i.e. between variables x and y. The law:

a) could be quadratic i.e. $y = px^2 + q$ or

b) could be of a reciprocal form i.e. $y = \dfrac{a}{x} + b$

where a, b, p and q are constants.

As a scientist you need to confirm the law by drawing an appropriate graph and finding the unknown constants. To do this we compare the laws with the **equation of a straight line** $Y = MX + C$, where M is the gradient and C is the y-intercept.

Example 4

The table gives the values of the variables x and y which are believed to be related by the law $y = px^2 + q$ where p and q are constants.

x	2	4	6	8	10
y	5	11	21	35	5

By drawing a suitable graph:

a) confirm the law is approximately correct.

b) find the values of the constants p and q, and state the law y, in terms of x.

Step 1 Compare the law with the equation of a straight line.
  i.e. $Y = MX + C$

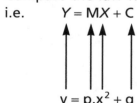

$y = p.x^2 + q$

Note $Y = MX + C$ is (variable) = (constant)(variable) + (constant). Constants must match with constants. Variables must match with variables.

So y is like Y, x^2 is like X, M = gradient = p and
C = y-intercept = q.
Hence plotting Y against X becomes plotting y against x^2.

Step 2 Construct a new table of
Y against X.

X	x^2	4	16	36	64	100
Y	y	5	11	21	35	53

Step 3 Plot a graph of Y against X, i.e. y against x^2.

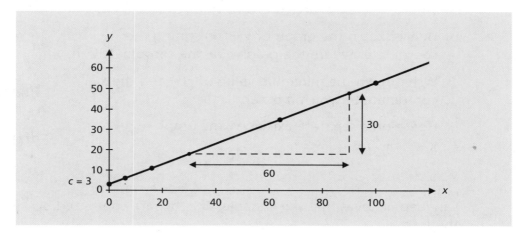

Looking at the scatter points one can see that they seem to lie on a
straight line. Hence the law $y = px^2 + q$ must indeed be true.

b) We draw a line of best fit on the graph (as shown). Then we use
this line to find the gradient and the intercept.

From the graph the intercept, C = 3 $\Longrightarrow$ q = 3
and the gradient M = $\frac{30}{60}$ = $\frac{1}{2}$ $\Longrightarrow$ p = $\frac{1}{2}$.

Hence the law is $y = 0.5x^2 + 3$.

Graphs

1 a) Express $f(x) = x^2 - 6x + 10$ in the form $f(x) = (x - a)^2 + b$, where 'a' and 'b' are constants to be determined.

Hints 1–2

b) Hence sketch the graph of $y = f(x)$ stating the coordinates where the graph cuts the coordinate axis.

Hints 3–4

c) Write down the minimum value of $f(x)$ and the x coordinate at which it occurs.

Hints 5–6

d) Hence on a separate axis draw the graph of $y = f(x + 3) + 4$.

Hints 7–8

2 Sandeep believes that the variables D and E are connected by the formula

$$E = \frac{p}{D} + q,$$

where 'p' and 'q' are constants.

By conducting some experiments he obtained the following results:

D	0.04	0.05	0.08	0.10	0.40
E	−2	0	3	4	7

a) By drawing a suitable graph confirm the law $E = \frac{p}{D} + q$ is true.

Hints 9–12

b) Find the constants p and q and state the law E, in terms of D.

Hints 13–17

Hints follow

Graphs

1   Use the algebra technique of 'completing the square' or 'comparing coefficients'.

2   Remember to state the constants 'a' and 'b'.

3   How is $f(x)$ in part a) been transformed from the basic graph of $y = x^2$?

4   To work out where $f(x)$ cuts the y-axis put $x = 0$ into the equation.

5   The minimum value of $f(x)$ is the y-value at the bottom of your curve in (b).

6   State the x-value at the bottom of the curve.

7   What does $f(x + 2) - 3$ do to the curve in part b)?

8   The curve in b) should be translated in two directions.

9   Write

$$E = \frac{p}{D} + q \qquad \text{as} \qquad E = p \times \frac{1}{D} + q$$

to help you.

10 Compare your law with the line $Y = MX + C$.

11 What letters are Y and X like?

12 Do the scatter points that you plot on your graph lie on a straight line?

13 Draw the line of best fit onto your graph.

14 Work out the gradient M and the intercept C.

15 Watch out!! The gradient is negative!!

16 Which letter is M like? Which letter is C like?

17 Substitute the values of the constants p and q into

$$E = \frac{p}{D} + q.$$

Answers on page 92

Mock examination paper

2 hours

1 In the diagram *C* is the centre of the
   circle and *AD* is a tangent to the circle
   at *A*.

   a) Find angle *ACB*.

   b) Given that the circle has radius
       8 cm, find:

       i)   The length *AB*.

       ii) The area of triangle *ABC*.

   c) A metal prism of length 20 cm is made
       with triangle *ABC* as its cross-section. Find the volume of the prism.

   d) The metal used to make the prism is melted down and used to
       make a cylinder of height 8 cm. Find the radius of the cylinder.

2 a) Factorise $2x^2 - 9x + 4$.

   b) Using an appropriate scale, draw the graph of $y = 2x^2 - 9x + 4$ for
       values of *x* between 0 and 5, showing the points where it crosses
       the *x*-axis and *y*-axis.

   c) Using your graph:

       i)   Write down the values of *x* for which $2x^2 - 9x + 4 > 0$.

       ii) Find the solutions to $2x^2 - 9x + 2 = 0$ correct to one decimal place.

3 a) Express $0.1\dot{6}\dot{2}$ as a fraction in its lowest terms.

   b) Salima approximates $0.1\dot{6}\dot{2}$ as 0.162.

       i)   Express 0.162 as a fraction in its lowest terms.

       ii) Find the size of the error Salima makes when she uses this
            approximation, expressing your answer as a fraction in its
            lowest term.

4 a) Gill had trained her dog to fetch a stick and decided to keep records of the dog's ability (because she was like that!). She recorded the following retrieval times:

2.3 sec, 2.1 sec, 2.7 sec, 1.9 sec, 2.0 sec, 2.1 sec.

Calculate to three decimal places the mean and the standard deviation of these times.

b) Later, Gill was told that she did not use her stopwatch correctly. She had overstated each time by 0.5 sec.

Without using your calculator, find the mean and standard deviation of the true times.

5 Solve the following equations:

a) $2^{3x} = \frac{1}{64}$ b) $\dfrac{\sqrt{(2x^3)}}{x^{0.5}} = \sqrt{8}$ c) $x^{1.5} = 27$.

6 Kevin finds 70 % of maths questions hard and the remainder easy. He has a probability of 0.4 of getting a hard question right, and a probability of 0.5 of getting an easy question right.

a) Show that the probability Kevin gets a randomly selected maths question right is 0.43.

b) If Kevin tries two questions, what is the probability he gets them both right?

c) When Kevin is given a test of N questions the probability he gets **at least one** right is 0.894 (to 3 d.p.).

i)   Write down the probability he gets **none** right.

ii)   By trial and improvement, find the value of N.

7 Tara walks 60 m at x metres per second. She then runs 80 m at $4x - 2$ metres per second.

a) Show that the total time Tara takes is $\dfrac{60}{x} + \dfrac{80}{4x - 2}$ seconds.

b) Given that Tara took 1 minute in total, solve this equation to find the possible values of x and explain why one of them is not a sensible solution.

8 Cone *A* and cone *B* are mathematically similar.

   The volume of cone *A* is 500 cm³ and the volume of cone *B* is 1500 cm³.

   The height of cone *B* is 30 cm. Calculate:

   a) The radius of cone *B*.

   b) The radius of cone *A* giving your answer to three significant figures.

9 *ABC* is a right-angled triangle such
   that the hypotenuse *AC* = 14 cm is
   correct to the nearest 2 cm and
   BC = 10 cm is correct to the nearest
   centimetre.

   Find the upper and lower bounds of
   the length of *AB* in centimetres.

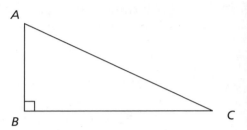

10 The diagram shows a side view of a wooden stand *ABCDE*, where *AB* is
   parallel to *DE*.

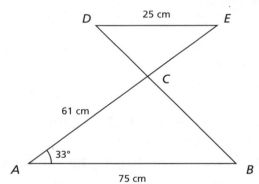

   a) Prove that the triangle *ABC* is similar to triangle *CDE*.

   b) Find the length of the side *CE*.

   c) Hence find the length of the side *CD*, leaving your answer to three
      significant figures.

11 Below is the graph of $y = \cos x$ for $-360° \leqslant x \leqslant 360°$.

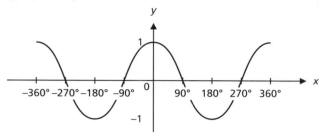

One solution of $\cos x = 0.89$ is $x = 27°$, correct to the nearest degree. Using the graph of $y = \cos x$ and its properties, find all the solutions of $\cos x = 0.89$ for $-360° \leqslant x \leqslant 360°$, giving your answers to the nearest degree.

12 The diagram shows the cone *VAB*, which has base diameter of 20 cm and has a slope length of 30 cm.

Find the volume of the cone, giving your answer correct to three significant figures.

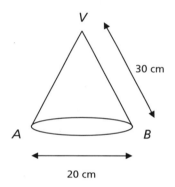

13 The diagram shows the side view of Ken's bread bin *OAB*, which is made from metal and wood. The side view is a quarter of a circle, centre *O* and radius *r* cm. The region shaded in the diagram is made from metal.

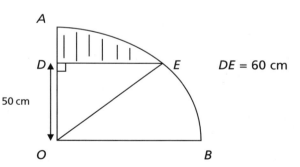

a) Calculate the radius *OB*.

b) Hence calculate the total area of the side of the bread bin, *OAB*.

c) Hence calculate shaded area in the diagram, giving your answer to three significant figures.

Answers on page 92

Answers to

Use your knowledge tests

Algebra

1 a) $a = 6; b = 1; c = -1 \Rightarrow x = \dfrac{-1 \pm \sqrt{[(1)^2 - 4 \times 6 \times -1]}}{2 \times 6} = \dfrac{-1 \pm \sqrt{[25]}}{2 \times 6} = \dfrac{-1 \pm 5}{12}$

So $x = \frac{1}{3}$ or $x = -\frac{1}{2}$
So we get $(x - \frac{1}{3})(x - -\frac{1}{2}) \Rightarrow (x - \frac{1}{3})(x + \frac{1}{2})$
$(x - \frac{1}{3}) \times 3 \Rightarrow (3x - 1)(x + \frac{1}{2}) \times 2 \Rightarrow (2x + 1)$ so we have $(3x - 1)(2x + 1)$

b) Although this looks hard because it has x^3 in it, we are OK once we note we can take a factor of x out:
$6x^3 + x^2 - x = 0 \Rightarrow x[6x^2 + x - 1] = 0$. The expression in brackets is what we solved earlier! So we get
$x[6x^2 + x - 1] = 0 \Rightarrow x(3x - 1)(2x + 1) = 0$ so $x = 0$ or $x = \frac{1}{3}$ or $x = -\frac{1}{2}$

2 a) $\dfrac{1}{2(x - 1)} - \dfrac{1}{2(x + 1)} = \dfrac{1[2(x + 1)] - 1[2(x - 1)]}{2(x - 1)2(x + 1)} = \dfrac{2x + 2 - 2x + 2}{4(x - 1)(x + 1)} = \dfrac{4}{4(x - 1)(x + 1)} = \dfrac{1}{(x - 1)(x + 1)} = \dfrac{1}{x^2 - 1}$

b) $\dfrac{1}{2(x - 1)} - \dfrac{1}{2(x + 1)} = \dfrac{1}{8} \Rightarrow \dfrac{1}{x^2 - 1} = \dfrac{1}{8}$

Cross-multiplying: $1 \times 8 = 1 \times (x^2 - 1) \Rightarrow 8 = x^2 - 1 \Rightarrow x^2 - 9 = 0$
$x^2 - 9 \equiv (x)^2 - (3)^2 \equiv (x - 3)(x + 3)$
So $x^2 - 9 = 0 \Rightarrow (x - 3)(x + 3) = 0 \Rightarrow x = 3, -3$

3 a) Perimeter $= 2 \times$ length $+ 2 \times$ width $\Rightarrow 2L + 2W = 52 \Rightarrow 2W = 52 - 2L \Rightarrow W = 26 - L$
b) Area $= L \times W \Rightarrow LW = 144$
c) We know $W = 26 - L$. so $L \times W = 144 \Rightarrow L \times (26 - L) = 144 \Rightarrow 26L - L^2 = 144 \Rightarrow L^2 - 26L + 144 = 0$
Solving:

$a = 1; b = -26; c = 144 \Rightarrow L = \dfrac{--26 \pm \sqrt{[(-26)^2 - 4 \times 1 \times 144]}}{2 \times 1} = \dfrac{26 \pm 10}{2}$

So $L = 18$ or 8
If $L = 18$, $W = 26 - 18 = 8$
If $L = 8$, $W = 26 - 8 = 18$ – this is wrong, since length must be more than width so $L = 18$ feet

4 Substituting: $5 = 20t + \frac{1}{2}(-9.8)t^2 \Rightarrow 5 = 20t - 4.9t^2$
Re-arranging: $4.9t^2 - 20t + 5 = 0. \Rightarrow a = 4.9; b = -20; c = 5$
So

$t = \dfrac{--20 \pm \sqrt{(-20)^2 - 4 \times 4.9 \times 5]}}{2 \times 4.9} = \dfrac{--20 \pm \sqrt{[400 - 98]}}{2 \times 4.9} = \dfrac{20 \pm \sqrt{302}}{9.8} \Rightarrow t = 3.81, 0.27$

5 i) $3 \times 3 \times 3 \times 3 = 81$, so $81 = 3^4$ so $\dfrac{1}{81} = \dfrac{1}{3^4} = 3^{-4}$

ii) $9^y = (3^2)^y = 3^{2y}$ so $3 \times 9^y = 3^1 \times 3^{2y} = 3^{2y + 1}$
iii) $27^y = (3^3)^y = 3^{3y}$ so $27 \times 27^y = 3^3 \times 3^{3y} = 3^{3y + 3}$

6 a) $x^{2/3} = 9 \Rightarrow \sqrt[3]{x^2} = 9 \Rightarrow x^2 = 9^3 = 729 \Rightarrow x = \sqrt{729} = 27$

b) $x^{-3} = 64 \Rightarrow \dfrac{1}{x^3} = 64 \Rightarrow x^3 = \dfrac{1}{64} \Rightarrow x = \sqrt[3]{\dfrac{1}{64}} = \dfrac{1}{4}$

7 a) Let x be the number. Then $3x + 5 < 50$ and $60 - 2x < 36$.

b) $3x + 5 < 50 \Rightarrow 3x < 45 \Rightarrow x < 15$

$60 - 2x < 36 \Rightarrow -2x < -24 \Rightarrow x > 12$

c) 13, 14

Rational and irrational numbers

1 Let $x = 0.213213213....$ Then $1000x = 213.213213213...$ so $999x = 213$ so $x = \frac{213}{999} = \frac{71}{333}$

2 a) $(6 + 2\sqrt{3})(6 - 2\sqrt{3}) = 36 - 12\sqrt{3} + 12\sqrt{3} - 2\sqrt{3} \times 2\sqrt{3} = 36 - 4 \times 3 = 24$

b) $(\sqrt{7} + \sqrt{5})(\sqrt{7} - \sqrt{5}) = (\sqrt{7})^2 - (\sqrt{5})^2 = 7 - 5 = 2$

c) $\dfrac{1}{2 + \sqrt{6}} \times \dfrac{2 + \sqrt{6}}{1} = 1,$ or $\dfrac{1}{2 + \sqrt{6}} \times \dfrac{1}{2 - \sqrt{6}} = \dfrac{1}{-2}$

3 $\sqrt{2} = 1.414...$ $\sqrt{3} = 1.732...$ so rational in between is 1.5

$(\sqrt{2})^2 = 2$ $(\sqrt{3})^2 = 3$ Try 2.5: $\sqrt{2.5} = 1.5811...$ so irrational, so $\sqrt{2.5}$ will do.

4 a) T, because when we add a fraction to a fraction, we always get a fraction, i.e. another rational number

b) F, e.g. $2 \times \sqrt{3} = 2\sqrt{3}$ is irrational

c) S: $\sqrt{2} \times \sqrt{3} = \sqrt{(2 \times 3)} = \sqrt{6}$, which is irrational, sometimes false: $\sqrt{2} \times 3\sqrt{2} = 6$.

d) S: $2\pi - \pi = \pi$, which is irrational, sometimes false: $(5 + \sqrt{2}) - (2 + \sqrt{2}) = 3$.

e) S: $(\sqrt{3})^2 = 3$, sometimes false: $(2 + \sqrt{3})^2 = (2 + \sqrt{3})(2 + \sqrt{3}) = 4 + 2\sqrt{3} + 2\sqrt{3} + 3 = 7 + 4\sqrt{3}$.

f) T: when one fraction is subtracted from another, the answer is always a fraction.

Accuracy in calculations and dimensions

1 a) Halve accuracy $\Rightarrow 3/2 = 1.5$ cm^3 UB $= 330 + 1.5 = 331.5$ cm^3

LB $= 330 - 1.5 = 328.5$ cm^3.

b) Diameter measured to one d.p. $\Rightarrow 0.1/2 = 0.05$. Hence for diameter UB $= 6.1 + 0.05 = 6.15$ and LB $= 6.1 - 0.05 = 6.05$.

$d = 2r \Rightarrow r = \dfrac{d}{2}.$ $V = \pi r^2 h = \pi\left(\dfrac{d}{2}\right)^2 h.$ So $V = \dfrac{\pi d^2 h}{4}.$

Re-arranging to make h the subject gives $h = \dfrac{4V}{\pi d^2}.$

UB for $h = \dfrac{4 \times 331.5}{\pi \times 6.05^2} = 11.5314...$cm, LB for $h = \dfrac{4 \times 328.5}{\pi \times 6.15^2} = 11.0585...$cm.

c) UB error $= 11.5314... - 11.2918... = 0.2396...$cm,

LB error $= 11.2918... - 11.0585... = 0.2333...$cm

$\Rightarrow$ Maximum possible error $= 0.2396...$cm

2 a) $\dfrac{1}{2}\pi r^2$ b) $\dfrac{4}{5}x(3y + z)$ c) $\dfrac{5}{6}\pi ab.$

Speed, distance and time

1 a) By drawing a tangent, obtain 10.2 m/s.

b) Zero, since curve is flat there.

c) This is the height at point A, which is 20.5 m.

d) Since the height becomes negative, it is falling below the level of the top of the cliff.

e) Goes up 20.5, down 20.5 m (to level with cliff) then down 22.5 m (below top of cliff) so total $= 20.5 + 20.5 + 22.5 = 63.5$ m.

Circle theorems

1 a) $a = 30°$ (alternate angles) $b = 90°$ (angle in a semicircle) $c = 60°$ (angles in a triangle sum to 180°) $d = 90°$ (angle in a semicircle) $e = 120°$ (opposite angle c in a cyclic quadrilateral)

b) Since $a + c = 90°$, all of its angles are 90°, so it is a rectangle.

2 a) Reflex angle $\angle COA = 220°$ (360° in a full circle) so $\angle CBA = 110°$ (angle at centre = twice angle at circumference).

b) $\angle DBA = 90°$ (angle in semicircle) $\angle CBA = 110°$ $\angle DBC = \angle CBA - \angle DBA = 20°$

c) i) $\angle BDC = \angle DBC = 20°$ ii) $\angle BCD = 180° - 40° = 140°$

d) $\angle DAB = 40°$, since $\angle DAB$ and $\angle BCD$ are opposite angles in a cyclic quadrilateral

e) $\angle ECB = \angle BDC = 20°$ (alternate segment theorem)

Trigonometry

1 Angle $A\hat{D}B = 180 - 47 = 133°$ hence angle $B\hat{A}C = 180 - (133 + 35) = 12°$.

Hence

$$\frac{AD}{\sin 35} = \frac{4.5}{\sin 12} \Rightarrow AD = \frac{4.5}{\sin 12} \times \sin 35 = 12.4144...\text{m}$$

Then

$$\frac{AC}{12.4144...} = \sin 47 \Rightarrow AC = 12.4144... \times \sin 47° = 9.0793... = 9.08 \text{ m (3 s.f.)}$$

2 Angle $X\hat{W}Y = 180 - (35 + 40) = 105°$

Hence $\dfrac{WY}{\sin 35} = \dfrac{50}{\sin 105} \Rightarrow WY = \dfrac{50}{\sin 105} \times \sin 35 = 29.6905...\text{m}$

Draw a vertical line from W to Z the other side of the road. Hence WZ is the width of the road and triangle WZY is a right-angled triangle with right angle at Z.

So

$$\frac{WZ}{29.6905...} = \sin 40 \Rightarrow WZ = 29.6905... \times \sin 40 = 19.08... = 19.1 \text{ m (3 s.f.)}$$

Areas and volumes

1 a) Drawing a complete diagram gives:

OY = 9 – 3 = 6cm. OZ = OX = radius = 9 cm

Angle $Y\hat{O}Z \Rightarrow \cos Y\hat{O}Z = \frac{6}{9}$

$\Rightarrow$ Angle $Y\hat{O}Z = \cos^{-1}(\frac{6}{9}) = 48.1897...$

Hence angle $X\hat{O}Z = 2 \times 48.1897... = 96.379...°$

Area shaded $= \dfrac{\pi r^2 x}{360} - \frac{1}{2} r^2 \sin X\hat{O}Z = \dfrac{\pi \times 9^2 \times 96.379}{360} - \frac{1}{2} \times 9^2 \times \sin(96.379)$

$= 27.877... = 27.9 \text{ cm}^2 \text{ (3 s.f.)}.$

b) Volume $= 27.877... \times 10$

$= 278.77..\text{cm}^3 = 279 \text{ cm}^3 (3 \text{ s.f.})$

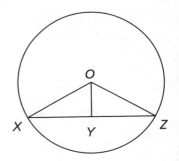

2 Height of cone $= \sqrt{11.5^2 - 6^2} = \sqrt{96.25} = 9.8107...$cm.

Volume of cone $= \frac{1}{3} \pi r^2 h = \frac{1}{3} \times \pi \times 6^2 \times 9.8107... = 369.855...\text{cm}^3.$

Height of cylinder $= 24 - 9.8107... = 14.1893...$cm.

Volume of cylinder $= \pi r^2 h = \pi \times 6^2 \times 14.1893... = 1604.772...\text{cm}^3.$

Hence volume of toy $= 1604.772... + 369.855... = 1974.627...\text{cm}^3.$

So volume of toy $= 1970\text{cm}^3 \text{ (3 s.f.)}.$

Proportion and similar shapes

1 $v \propto \dfrac{1}{\sqrt{y}} \Rightarrow v = \dfrac{k}{\sqrt{y}}$ $1500 = \dfrac{k}{\sqrt{4}} \Rightarrow k = 1500 \times 2 = 3000$ So $v = \dfrac{3000}{\sqrt{y}}$

When $v = 500$, we have

$$500 = \frac{3000}{\sqrt{y}} \Rightarrow \sqrt{y} = \frac{3000}{500} = 6. \text{ So } y = 6^2 = 36 \text{ years.}$$

2 $E \propto x^2 \Rightarrow E = kx^2$ so $E = k(4)^2 \Rightarrow E = 16k$ ①.

Energy doubled gives us $2E$ so $2E = kx^2$ ②.

Substituting ① into ② gives $2(16k) = kx^2 \Rightarrow 32k = kx^2$.

Cancelling the ks gives $x^2 = 32 \Rightarrow x = \sqrt{32} = 5.65685...$ Energy has doubled when the elastic band has extended 5.66 cm (2 d.p.) so further extension = 5.66 – 4 = 1.66 cm.

3 **a)** $L_{Big} = kL_{small} \Rightarrow 15 = k(12) \Rightarrow k = 15/12 = 1.25$

  $V_{Big} = k^3 V_{small} \Rightarrow 600 = (1.25)^3 V_{Small} \Rightarrow V_{Small} = \dfrac{600}{(1.25)^3} = 307.2 \text{ cm}^3$

b) Ratio of areas $= k^2 = (1.25)^2 = 1.5625$ so ratio of areas = 1.5625 : 1

Vectors

1 a) i) $\overrightarrow{OC} = \overrightarrow{OB} + \overrightarrow{BC} = \mathbf{b} + 3\mathbf{a} = 3\mathbf{a} + \mathbf{b}$.
  ii) $\overrightarrow{AB} = \overrightarrow{AO} + \overrightarrow{OB} = -\mathbf{a} + \mathbf{b}$.
  iii) $\overrightarrow{AC} = \overrightarrow{AB} + \overrightarrow{BC} = -\mathbf{a} + \mathbf{b} + 3\mathbf{a} = 2\mathbf{a} + \mathbf{b}$.
  iv) $\overrightarrow{OR} = \overrightarrow{OA} + \overrightarrow{AR} \Rightarrow$ We need to find $\overrightarrow{AR}$. Since $\overrightarrow{AR} : \overrightarrow{RB} = 1 : 3$ then $\overrightarrow{AR} = \frac{1}{4}\overrightarrow{AB} = \frac{1}{4}(-\mathbf{a} + \mathbf{b})$ so
  $\overrightarrow{OR} = \mathbf{a} + \frac{1}{4}(-\mathbf{a} + \mathbf{b}) = \mathbf{a} - \frac{1}{4}\mathbf{a} + \frac{1}{4}\mathbf{b} = \frac{3}{4}\mathbf{a} + \frac{1}{4}\mathbf{b}$.
  v) $\overrightarrow{RC} = \overrightarrow{RO} + \overrightarrow{OC} = -(\frac{3}{4}\mathbf{a} + \frac{1}{4}\mathbf{b}) + 3\mathbf{a} + \mathbf{b} = -\frac{3}{4}\mathbf{a} - \frac{1}{4}\mathbf{b} + 3\mathbf{a} + \mathbf{b} = \frac{9}{4}\mathbf{a} + \frac{3}{4}\mathbf{b}$
  b) $\overrightarrow{RC} = \frac{9}{4}\mathbf{a} + \frac{3}{4}\mathbf{b} = 3(\frac{3}{4}\mathbf{a} + \frac{1}{4}\mathbf{b}) = 3\overrightarrow{RO}$. Since $\overrightarrow{RC}$ is a multiple of the vector $\overrightarrow{OR}$ then $\overrightarrow{OR}$ and $\overrightarrow{RC}$ are parallel vectors.
  c) Since $\overrightarrow{OR}$ and $\overrightarrow{RC}$ are parallel vectors and the point R is common to both vectors then it can be deduced that the points O, R and C lie on the same line (i.e. they are collinear).

2 a) A triangle ABC should be drawn where AB = 14 knots, BC = 6 knots and angle ABC = 135° (i.e. 90° + 45°) and the actual speed is represented by edge AC and the direction is the angle BAC.
  b) Using cosine rule $AC^2 = 14^2 + 6^2 - 2(14)(6)\cos 135° = 350.7939... \Rightarrow AC = 18.729...\text{knots}$.

  c) Using cosine rule $\cos B\hat{A}C = \dfrac{14^2 + (18.729...)^2 - 6^2}{2 \times 14 \times 18.729...} = 0.97401...$
  $\Rightarrow$ Bearing = angle $B\hat{A}C = \cos^{-1}(0.97401...) = 13.1°$ (3 s.f.)

Probability and statistics

1 a) Need YYY or BBB but YYY is impossible, since there are only 2 yellows (so its probability is 0).
  $P(BBB) = \frac{6}{8} \times \frac{5}{7} \times \frac{4}{6} = \frac{5}{14}$.
  b) P(at least 1 yellow) = 1 – P(no yellows)
  = 1 – P(all black) = $1 - \frac{5}{14} = \frac{9}{14}$.
  c) We need YBB, BYB and BBY:
  $P(YBB) = \frac{2}{8} \times \frac{6}{7} \times \frac{5}{6} = \frac{5}{28}$ $P(BYB) = \frac{6}{8} \times \frac{2}{7} \times \frac{5}{6} = \frac{5}{28}$
  $P(BBY) = \frac{6}{8} \times \frac{5}{7} \times \frac{2}{6} = \frac{5}{28}$
  So $P(\text{one yellow}) = \frac{5}{28} + \frac{5}{28} + \frac{5}{28} = \frac{15}{28}$.

2 a) P(all tails) = P(no heads)
  = 1 – P(at least one head) = $1 - \frac{31}{32} = \frac{1}{32}$.
  b) Try out values:
  1 toss: P(all tails) = $\frac{1}{2}$
  2 tosses: P(all tails) = $\frac{1}{2} \times \frac{1}{2} = \frac{1}{4}$
  3 tosses: P(all tails) = $\frac{1}{2} \times \frac{1}{2} \times \frac{1}{2} = \frac{1}{8}$
  4 tosses: P(all tails) = $\frac{1}{2} \times \frac{1}{2} \times \frac{1}{2} \times \frac{1}{2} = \frac{1}{16}$
  5 tosses: P(all tails) = $\frac{1}{2} \times \frac{1}{2} \times \frac{1}{2} \times \frac{1}{2} \times \frac{1}{2} = \frac{1}{32}$
  So $N = 5$

3 i) mean $= \dfrac{-15 + -10 + -5 + 0 + 5 + 10 + 15}{7} = 0$

  SD: mean$^2 = 0$ $(-15)^2 = 225$ $(-10)^2 = 100$
  $(-5)^2 = 25$ $0^2 = 0$ $5^2 = 25$ $10^2 = 100$
  $15^2 = 225$
  $\dfrac{225 + 100 + 25 + 0 + 25 + 100 + 225}{7} = 100$
  $100 - 0 = 100$ $\sqrt{100} = 10$
  So SD = 10
  ii) Mean = $0 \div 3 = 0$ SD = $10 \div 3 = \frac{10}{3} = 3\frac{1}{3}$

  iii) Mean = $0 \times a = 0$; SD = $\dfrac{10}{3} \times a = \dfrac{10a}{3}$

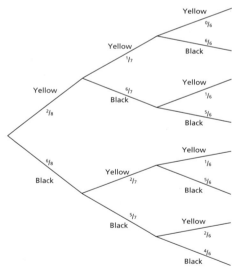

Graphs

1 a) Either completing the square: $f(x) = x^2 - 6x + 10 = (x-3)^2 - 9 + 10 = (x-3)^2 + 1$
   Hence $a = 3$ and $b = 1$.
   Or comparing terms:
   $f(x) = (x-a)^2 + b = (x-a)(x-a) + b = x^2 - ax - ax + a^2 + b$
   $= x^2 - 2ax + a^2 + b \equiv x^2 - 6x + 10$.

   Comparing x terms $\Rightarrow -2a = -6 \Rightarrow a = \dfrac{-6}{-2} = 3$.

   Comparing constant terms $\Rightarrow a^2 + b = 10 \Rightarrow 3^2 + b = 10 \Rightarrow b = 10 - 9 = 1$
   Hence $f(x) = (x-3)^2 + 1$.

   b) From part a), the graph of $y = x^2$ has been translated $\begin{pmatrix} 3 \\ 1 \end{pmatrix}$.

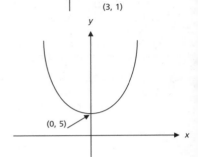

   When $x = 0$, $y = 0^2 - 6(0) + 10 = 10 \Rightarrow$ Cuts y-axis at $(0, 10)$.
   c) The minimum value is $f(x) = 1$ and this occurs when $x = 3$.
   d) The graph in part b) is translated by the translation
   vector $\begin{pmatrix} -3 \\ 4 \end{pmatrix}$.

2 a) Writing $E = \dfrac{p}{D} + q$ as: $E = p \times \dfrac{1}{D} + q$

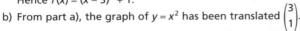

   $Y = M \quad X + C$

   and comparing with $Y = MX + C$, implies that we plot E against $\dfrac{1}{D}$.

$1/D$	25	20	12.5	10	2.5
E	-2	0	3	4	7

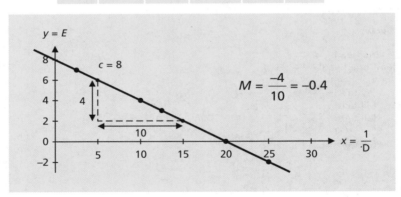

$M = \dfrac{-4}{10} = -0.4$

   Since the scatter points seem to lie on a straight line then the law $E = \dfrac{p}{D} + q$ is true.
   b) Using your graph the gradient $M = p \approx -0.4$, and the intercept
   $C = q \approx 8$.

   Hence $E = -\dfrac{0.4}{D} + 8$.

Mock examination paper

1 a) Angle $B\hat{A}C = 50°$ (angle between radius and tangent $= 90°$). Since triangle ABC is isosceles (since $AC = BC =$ radius), $\angle ABC = 50°$ so $\angle ACB = 180 - 100 = 80°$.

b) Since triangle is isosceles, we have
   i) $AB = 2 \times 8 \sin 40 = 10.28$ cm
   ii) Need height of triangle $= 8 \cos 40 = 6.13$ cm
   So area $= \frac{1}{2} \times 10.28 \times 6.13 = 31.5$ cm^2
c) Volume $= 31.5 \times 20 = 630$ cm^2
d) Volume $= 630$ cm$^2 = \pi r^2 h = \pi r^2 \times 8$ So
   $r^2 = 630 \div (8\pi) = 25.07$ cm$^2 \Rightarrow r = 5.0$ cm

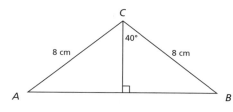

2 a) $a = 2 \quad b = -9 \quad c = 4 \Rightarrow x = \dfrac{-9 \pm \sqrt{[(-9)^2 - 4 \times 2 \times 4]}}{2 \times 2} = \dfrac{9 \pm \sqrt{[49]}}{4} = 4, \frac{1}{2}$

So we have $(x - 4)(x - \frac{1}{2}) \Rightarrow (x - 4)(2x - 1)$

b)

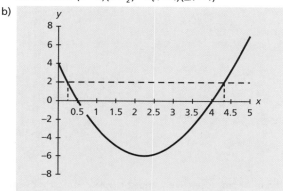

c) i) This is when it is above x-axis so $x < 0.5$ and $x > 4$
   ii) $2x^2 - 9x + 2 = 0 \Rightarrow (2x^2 - 9x + 4) - 2 = 0 \Rightarrow 2x^2 - 9x + 4 = 2 \Rightarrow x = 0.2$ and $x = 4.3$ (1 d.p.)

3 a) $x = 0.1626262\ldots \Rightarrow 100x = 16.2626262\ldots$

   $\Rightarrow 100x - x = 16.2626262\ldots - 0.1626262 \Rightarrow 99x = 16.1 \Rightarrow x = \dfrac{16.1}{99} = \frac{161}{990}$

b) i) $0.162 = \frac{162}{1000} = \frac{81}{500}$

   ii) Error $= \dfrac{161}{990} - \dfrac{81}{500} = \dfrac{50 \times 161 - 99 \times 81}{49500} = \dfrac{8050 - 8019}{49500} = \dfrac{31}{49500}$

4 a) Mean $= \dfrac{2.3 + 2.1 + 2.7 + 1.9 + 2.0 + 2.1}{6} = \dfrac{13.1}{6}$
           $= 2.18333\ldots = 2.183$ sec (3 d.p.)

   Standard deviation $= \sqrt{\left(\dfrac{2.3^2 + 2.1^2 + 2.7^2 + 1.9^2 + 2.0^2 + 2.1^2}{6}\right) - (2.183\ldots)^2}$
                  $= 0.26087\ldots$
   Hence standard deviation $= 0.261$ sec (3 d.p.)
b) True mean $= 2.183 - 0.5 = 1.683$ sec. True standard deviation is the same $= 0.261$ sec.

5 a) $64 = 2 \times 2 \times 2 \times 2 \times 2 \times 2 = 2^6$ so $\frac{1}{64} = 2^{-6}$ So $2^{3x} = 2^{-6} \Rightarrow 3x = -6 \Rightarrow x = -2$
b) $\sqrt{(2x^3)} = \sqrt{2}\sqrt{(x^3)} = 2^{0.5}(x^3)^{0.5} = 2^{0.5}x^{1.5}$
   so $2^{0.5}x^{1.5} \div x^{0.5} = 2^{0.5}x^{1.5 - 0.5} = 2^{0.5}x^1 = \sqrt{2} \times x$
   So $\sqrt{2x} = \sqrt{8} \Rightarrow x = \sqrt{8} \div \sqrt{2} = 2$
c) $x^{1.5} = \sqrt{(x^3)} = 27 \Rightarrow x^3 = 27^2 = 729 \Rightarrow x = \sqrt[3]{729} = 9$

6 a) P(right) $= 0.7 \times 0.4 + 0.3 \times 0.5 = 0.28 + 0.15 = 0.43$
b) $0.43 \times 0.43 = 0.1849$
c) i) $1 - 0.894 = 0.106$
   ii) P(none right) = P(all wrong) $= 0.57 \times 0.57 \times \ldots \times 0.57$ (N times) $= 0.57^N$
Try $N = 5$: $0.57^5 = 0.060$ (too small)
$N = 3$: $0.57^3 = 0.185$ (too big)
$N = 4$: $0.57^4 = 0.106$
So $N = 4$

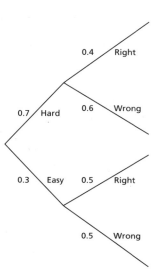

93

7 a) Time = distance ÷ speed so time walking = $60 \div x$ and time running = $80 \div (4x - 2)$ So total time = $\dfrac{60}{x} + \dfrac{80}{4x - 2}$

b) We have $\dfrac{60}{x} + \dfrac{80}{4x - 2} = 60$

So $\dfrac{60(4x - 2) + 80x}{x(4x - 2)} = 60 \Rightarrow \dfrac{320x - 120}{x(4x - 2)} = 60 \Rightarrow 320x - 120 = 60x(4x-2)$

So $320x - 120 = 240x^2 - 120x \Rightarrow 240x^2 - 440x + 120 = 0 \Rightarrow 6x^2 - 11x + 3 = 0$

So

$x = \dfrac{11 \pm \sqrt{[(-11)^2 - 4 \times 6 \times 3]}}{2 \times 6} = \dfrac{11 \pm \sqrt{[121 - 72]}}{12} = \dfrac{11 \pm 7}{12} = 1\frac{1}{2}, \frac{1}{3}$

But it can't be $\frac{1}{3}$ since then $4x - 2$ would be negative so $x = 1\frac{1}{2}$

8 a) For cone B, $V = \dfrac{1}{3}\pi r^2 h \Rightarrow 1500 = \dfrac{1}{3}\pi r^2(30) \Rightarrow r^2 = \dfrac{3 \times 1500}{\pi(30)}$

Hence $r = \sqrt{\dfrac{3 \times 1500}{\pi(30)}} = 6.90988...\text{cm}$

b) $V_{Big} = k^3 V_{Small} \Rightarrow V_B = k^3 V_A \Rightarrow 1500 = k^3(500) \Rightarrow k^3 = \dfrac{1500}{500} = 3$

So $k = \sqrt[3]{3} = 1.44225...$ Also $L_{Big} = kL_{Small} \Rightarrow 6.90988... = 1.44225...L_{Small}$

$L_{Small} = \dfrac{6.90988...}{1.44225...} = 4.79104... = 4.79 \text{ cm (3 s.f.)}$

9 The upper and lower bounds for AC are 15 cm and 13 cm respectively and the upper and lower bounds for BC are 11.5 cm and 10.5 cm respectively.

For AC: $UB = \sqrt{(15^2 - 9.5^2)} = \sqrt{134.75} = 11.6082...\text{cm}$
$LB = \sqrt{(13^2 - 10.5^2)} = \sqrt{58.75} = 7.6649...\text{cm}$

10 a) Angle $B\hat{A}C$ = Angle $D\hat{E}C$ because they are alternate angles.
Angle $D\hat{C}E$ = Angle $A\hat{C}B$ because they are opposite angles. Hence triangle ABC is similar to triangle CDE.

b) $\dfrac{CE}{61} = \dfrac{25}{75} \Rightarrow CE = \dfrac{25}{75} \times 61 = 20\frac{1}{3} \text{ cm}$

c) Note that angle $C\hat{E}D = 33°$ and hence use the cosine rule to find CD.
Hence $CD^2 = 25^2 + (20.3333...)^2 - 2(25)(20.3333...)\cos 33 = 185.7960...$
$CD = \sqrt{185.7960...} = 13.6307... = 13.6 \text{ cm (3 s.f.)}$

11 Draw the line $y = 0.85$ onto the graph of $y = \cos x$
i) $x = -360 + 27 = -333°$ ii) $x = 0 - 27 = -27°$ iii) $x = 27°$ (given) iv) $x = 360 - 27 = 333°$
Overall $x = \{-333°, -27°, 27°, 333°\}$

12 By Pythagoras, height = $\sqrt{30^2 - 10^2} = 28.2843...\text{cm}$.
Volume $V = \dfrac{1}{3}\pi r^2 h = \dfrac{1}{3}\pi(10^2)(28.2843...) = 2961.92... = 2960 \text{ cm}^3 \text{ (3 s.f.)}$

13 a) Radius OB = length $OE = \sqrt{60^2 + 50^2} = 78.1025...\text{cm}$
b) Area $OAB = \frac{1}{4}\pi r^2 = \frac{1}{4}\pi(78.1025...)^2 = 4790.929...\text{cm}^2$
c) Area triangle $ODE = \frac{1}{2}(50)(60) = 1500 \text{ cm}^2$

Let angle $D\hat{O}E = x° \Rightarrow \tan x = \dfrac{60}{50} \Rightarrow x = \tan^{-1}\left(\dfrac{60}{50}\right) = 50.1944...$

Angle $B\hat{O}E = 90 - 50.1944... = 39.8056...$

Area of sector $OBE = \dfrac{\pi(78.1025...)^2(39.8056...)}{360} = 2118.953...$

Area of $ODEB = 1500 + 2118.953... = 3618.953...$
∴ Shaded area = $4790.929... - 3618.953 = 1171.976... = 1170 \text{ cm}^2 \text{ (3 s.f.)}$